From Fears

To Freedom

The H₂G™ Revolution

Shawn Cassidy

The secret to growth, fulfillment and success

through trusted and meaningful relationships

Kathy & Russ —
I hope you are inspired by the
H₂G formula/message.
for your friendship!
Go Green! H₂G 365!
Thank you
Shawn

Printed in the United States of America.

First Printing, July 2013.

ISBN 978-0-9894347-2-0

Allura Press

Costa Mesa, CA

(www.allurapress.com)

Dedication

TEAM Cassidy

Mom and Dad:

Elizabeth "Betty" Cassidy and Colonel Brendan

"Hop" Cassidy, United States Marine Corps (Ret.)

My sisters and brother: Brenda, Belinda, Ann, Colleen, Kathy and Shane.

My wife: Ellena Cassidy and my kids, Jordan and Molly.

Disclaimer and copyright information

No part of this publication may be reproduced, distributed, or transmitted in any form or by any means, including photocopying, recording, or other electronic or mechanical methods, or by any information storage and retrieval system, without prior written permission from the publisher and author, except for brief quotations embodied in critical reviews and certain other noncommercial uses permitted by copyright law. For permission requests, write to the publisher at the address below.

The author and publisher assume neither liability nor responsibility to any person or entity with respect to any direct or indirect loss or damage caused, or alleged to be caused, by the information contained herein, or for errors, omissions, inaccuracies, or any other inconsistency within these pages, or for unintentional slights against any people or organizations.

Discrepancies with the perceived characters or any similarities to anyone living or dead, with similar names, circumstances, or history, are coincidental and unintentional.

Contents

H₂G

Introduction

In the fall of 1979 beginning my junior year in college at the University Of Southern California (USC), and at the height of the 1980 Presidential Elections, I became pre-occupied and obsessed with learning about *business* and *political* relationships. It intrigued me how important they were in understanding relationships in general.

During that time, I met a visiting professor who forever changed my life and the understanding of relationships, Dr. Herbert "Herb" Shepard. Little did I know at the time that Professor Shepard was one of the pioneers and leading experts in the country on human relationships and organizational development. Three years later in graduate school at USC, I took his life-changing course on that same subject.

After that experience, I couldn't get those ideas out of my head and they eventually led to what you are about to read.

I knew that even before meeting Professor Shepard, growing up in a large close knit military family, I was taught the importance of relationships, that your word is your bond and that trust isn't a given; it had to be earned. I had a mother and father who valued and supported **relationships** as **everything.**

Professor Shepard humbly lived that importance! I ended up writing and developing a project entitled "*The Relationship Ladder: 7 Steps to Understanding and Building the Trusted Relationship.*" His inspiration and encouragement have always stayed with me.

Being a student of personal and organizational development and leadership, I wanted to identify for myself what I thought were *the elements or steps to reaching the ultimate trusted relationship.* I thought that if a plan did not exist, I would create one.

Some 30 years later after graduating from USC, I ran into a professor who knew I had written the above piece in Dr. Shepard's class. One of the first things he said was, "Did you ever do anything with that idea? It was great."

First, I was shocked that he remembered, but more importantly, I was thrilled that he thought to ask. When I told him I had not, but had personally used my model over the years in business, he smiled and said, "You should consider sharing it and publishing it."

It's funny how serendipitous life is at times. That one chance encounter was the beginning of this book. In fact, that evening I went home and began to make notes. The further I got into the material, the more expansive it grew to include some of my own stories and experiences that have proven my model and new thinking on just how others can benefit.

Chapter One

State of the Art

In today's new exploding technology and information age, I don't think anyone would argue with the fascination, excitement and even the addiction of the tsunami of social media.

The benefits of technology are undeniable in nearly every aspect of our lives. How it affects us for the better is obvious: it makes every day easier, more comfortable, and accessible and allows for even greater discoveries faster than ever before.

What is NOT so obvious...but is becoming more so every day, is its *effect* on *human relationships.* (For every action good or bad, there is a reaction in the opposite direction; the light side, the dark side.)

Perhaps today's technology is "state of the art" but what it can't replace are our relationships, our bonds, the things that *really* matter, the things that make us human.

As I began to write this, I realized that our...
connected world...

...is actually becoming more and more

DISCONNECTED.

In other words, it's a double-edged sword. Technology has given us some **unbelievable** tools to instantly learn, share, grow and connect to the world and to see into the future. The problem and challenge is that it also often gives us the **FALSE SECURITY** of being intimate with each other, knowing so much about our family, friends and work colleagues, yet not really connecting us in the ways that only we are capable of **without any external tools**. Our emails, texts and the like are merely *transactions.*

In other words, **connecting through technology isn't the *best* we can do.** It *isn't* state of the art, at least not in the core human sense, not by a long shot.

This book is all about developing, creating, growing and nurturing trusted and meaningful relationships in every part of our lives and that is the area where technology and social media in particular are failing us. We are being lulled into a sense that we are actually growing closer together, when nothing could be further from the truth!

Look in any newspaper, browse the internet or watch television and it is almost impossible to escape the stories of what so many people, particularly the young, view as meaningful relationships. Take for example the recent national headline news story of the Notre Dame Football star, Manti Te'o. At first, it appeared he had either been duped or been a part of a very strange story. It later turned out that he had nothing to do with it, with the odd exception that this bright young man said, **"He fell in love with a girl through the internet!"**

2

To make matters even more complicated, this *girl* ended up being a young troubled and abused *man*.

I wonder what Manti thinks now about social media, about being connected? (Please, I am not judging this young man, merely using the extreme *real* example to illustrate one of my points.)

This promising, young scholar athlete with a high grade point average and a seemingly golden ticket to a very profitable NFL career **fell in love with a picture, voicemail messages, and the subsequent content that was posted on a fabricated twitter profile account. YIKES.**

This is the *state of the art* of some of our relationships or rather the connections in our world today where people are constantly tweeting, texting or emailing each other's every move, mood or the latest gossip about someone else. I find it ironic that the more "connected" we become, the further apart we often grow and the more superficial some of our relationships become. It's an easy way out of the *real* attention needed for *real* relationships to flourish.

There are more than seven billion people on the planet now and the more populated it becomes, the further apart we drift at once compressing in physical proximity, yet drifting apart emotionally.

Thanks to the internet and social media we can reach out via programs like Skype and see our family and friends from anywhere around the world. We can also now pretend to draw people to us as "friends" with similar "likes" but at the same time, hold them at bay on a human level while still appearing to maintain a relationship—*transactions*.

Not to take away for even a split second the incredible advances and opportunities that technology is providing us every minute of the day in every conceivable industry, profession or trade, but it begs the question: "Is all the face time glued to cell phones, tablets, computers and TV threatening and seriously competing with our quality personal time? Is it also threatening our ability to create and nurture real meaningful relationships? Are these wonderful and powerful tools distracting us and substituting "entertainment" and the briefest of "encounters" for the real thing?" Are we missing out and giving up on the real one-on-one time with our kids, spouses, partners, parents, grandparents, friends that we should be engaging in?

To be fair, it isn't the actual technology that is driving us apart, but the obsessive and addictive nature of instant gratification that pulls us. It promises the "semblance" of a "connect," a friend, a few moments when we are lonely. It assures us that we are a part of something and our opinions and feelings matter.

We buy into these *transactions* because no one wants to be lonely. Nobody wants to feel like he or she is on the outside looking in. Everyone wants to feel his or her opinion is valuable. Everyone wants to be a part of something. We all want to contribute to the dialogue...

...so we are pulled into a cyber-world, sometimes even anonymously and away from the reality of the things that are truly important to us—real people, *real* relationships.

We've all had challenges from broken marriages, business failures, personal financial hardships, impossible schedules, disjointed families, haunting addictions—the list is practically endless. No one is left untouched in some way.

With all these challenges, and the ultra-fast pace of life in general, the world's need for intelligent, clear, loving, **values-based relationships** is greater now than ever before in history! We're actually starving for it and don't even know it in many cases, because we are obsessed, desensitized and addicted to our new technological world.

If the addiction of transactional and on the fly technology driven relationships goes unchecked and untreated, in my humble opinion, you have the makings of a lost generation or more. Some of my close friends actually think we have already gone over the edge and it's too late. I disagree. While we may be hanging over the edge, we can't give up. We need a serious wakeup call to understand, manage and treat the technology addiction affecting our relationships worldwide. However, this book isn't about that one threat—technology…

…it's about the solution to all the challenges we face that dilute our **true emotional** contact with others and our opportunity and need to grow trusted and meaningful relationships. In addition, it's about a REVOLUTION in our daily attitudes and behaviors, a powerful 365 day a year plan to become what I call, AGENTS OF CHANGE.

My journey to writing this book began in that meeting with my old professor and culminated with an event that happened four years ago. This event changed my life forever and was really the spark that lit the fire in me to finish this book. Allow me a moment to tell you that story. It was a watershed moment in my life, but by no means the only disconnect and tragedy that set me on my quest.

My personal wakeup call

A sea change took place in my life that I want to share with you, a soul-opening event that forever changed the way I viewed my relationships.

Perhaps you have had one of these, an experience that could be called an epiphany, a life-altering event that took you by the shoulders, shook you to your marrow, slapped you in your mental face, and said, "This is your life test. What you do here and now will determine the course of the rest of your life, good or bad. You have this one chance to get it right, to get off your butt and change your entire perspective and to forever right your priorities and modify your behavior. You will never have a chance like this again and if you don't act and act appropriately, you may never forgive yourself."

This is my story:
March 24, 2009

It was 3:02 a.m. I was dead asleep at home when my cell phone vibrated on my bed stand. My first thought was, *this isn't good. 3:00 a.m. calls are rarely about good news.*

In that split second it took me to reach for the phone and see the familiar 310 area code, a shudder went down my spine, and my stomach curled up into a knot. I had a bad feeling, *this is trouble.*

"Hello. This is Shawn."

"Shawn, this is Al. I have terrible news I'm afraid."

Oh my God, I thought. *This is going to be horrible.* In less than two seconds, my body went into the fight or flight mode preparing for the worst, preparing for danger.

"What is it Al?" I said quickly wanting him to hurry.

"Jordan has gone into cardiac arrest and is in the ER at Gardena Memorial. The EMTs just left the house and pulled up to the hospital ER five minutes ago. Thank God they used the defibrillator on him."

I couldn't believe what I was hearing, though I knew based on the last few years of my son's life that it was true. That nightmare call that every parent fears had come. I still had the phone in the crook of my neck as I listened and rummaged through my closet for some clothes, pulling on a pair of jeans simultaneously.

Fear and adrenalin kicked in. My heart was beating so hard I thought it would pound through my chest; my brain was running on overdrive.

Al continued, "We don't have all the details Shawn, but Jordan has overdosed smoking heroin. We also found Vicodin and Xanax in his room that we believe he took. The ER doctor asked me to call and get you on the phone."

"Al, is he alive?"

"Shawn, I'm sorry, I don't know, he's in the operating room now. The doctor told me to get you on the phone ASAP."

After waiting nearly 45 seconds, which seemed like an eternity and with my heart pumping in my throat, the ER doctor came on.

"Mr. Cassidy, I understand Jordan Cassidy is your son, is that correct? "Yes. Yes." I wanted him to hurry his news.

"Jordan's condition is extremely critical. Where are you now?" He asked me as I gripped the phone so tight, I thought I was going to break it.

"I'm in San Diego. Is he going to make it?" I blurted out, slipping one arm through my shirt.

"How soon can you get here?" He asked as I looked around for my shoes.

I knew exactly how long it would take me. I had already visited Jordan many times during his stay at the adult sobriety house in Los Angeles.

"I'm 120 miles away doctor, a good hour and a half."

"Okay," he said and I could tell by the sound of that one word, that he was more than disappointed in my answer.

"Mr. Cassidy, just know that we are doing everything we can to stabilize and save Jordan. Your son arrived here with no heartbeat. He has a very low heart rate at 14 beats a minute along with a collapsed lung, so you need to get here as soon as you can."

"I need to know doctor, is he going to make it?" I blurted out again.

"Mr. Cassidy, we are doing everything we can. That is all I can tell you now. Honestly, I don't know if you will make it in time"

"I'm on my way," was all I said and I hung up the phone and was out the door in less than 30 seconds. I needed answers. I couldn't bear the thought of bringing this shocking and devastating news to my wife Ellena, not yet.

Throwing my shoes on the front seat and turning the ignition key my father's words came to me as they often do, "In a crisis or chaotic situation, you must remain calm, cool and collected if you want to survive."

Easy to say, I often thought, but after enough practice and hearing those words in my mind so many times over the years, it was much easier to calm myself, but not until after I said those words a few times.

The phone call had started that all too familiar cascade of bodily chemicals along with adrenalin flooding through my veins. My father knew about crisis and survival. He survived a near death gunshot wound at the age of 15 during a mass high school shooting in 1947 by some deranged man in New York. He had also survived four one-year combat tours in Vietnam as a Marine platoon officer and on top of all that, he survived cancer, so, his words resonated with me loud and clear.

Pulling my car onto the 5 Freeway in San Diego, Gardena seemed a long, long way, almost in another state. Merging into traffic, I sped up to 95 m.p.h. but then, using my father's advice, I managed to slow my heartbeat down, breathe deeply and think calmly. I slowed down to a freeway crawl of 60 m.p.h. as Jordan's entire childhood replayed like a home movie in my head.

I wouldn't be of any use to Jordan, if I didn't get to the hospital but I was not in a hurry to see him covered in a white sheet on a gurney either.

There were plenty of memories to occupy me with my prayers. I felt tears rolling down my cheeks as I merged onto the 405. I was not giving up! Hope, prayer and faith occupied my mind and heart every second of the drive.

I began reflecting and remembering all the great life experiences we had shared: swimming with the dolphins and stingray's in Cancun, touring the alligator and sea turtle farms in the Isle Mujeres, Mexico, visiting Winston Churchill's WWII bunker in London, touring the beautiful Highlands in

Scotland, cheering together in Yankee stadium at the World Series, coaching him in little league baseball for eight years, among many wonderful experiences.

I even remembered Jordan's first survival swim lessons when he was only two years old in our back yard swimming pool; teaching Jordan to body surf on the beach at Camp Pendleton military base in 1997, the same place where my father taught me to swim and body surf 30 years before.

I was flooded with the many great times together; the memories were endless. My mind flitted back and forth from questions, to memories to prayers. What went wrong? How did this wonderful little boy and smart handsome man end up so terribly wrong? Why did Jordan throw away eight months of sobriety? Why was he throwing away his life?

When was I going to tell Jordan's younger sister, Molly that she lost her brother and may need to withdraw from her first year of college (before she even started) to grieve for his passing death?

I needed to hold it together and have all the answers to prepare Ellena and Molly for a living nightmare. It wasn't fair for either of them. Ellena had worked so hard fighting for Jordan's sobriety over the past five years and Molly had worked hard to earn a college field hockey scholarship that was to pay for her college education.

She also strongly supported Jordan's battle with sobriety, which was not easy on her.

I cannot tell you how many emotions I experienced on that drive—from hope to anger, to hopelessness, to hope then on to empathy to forgiveness—all of it. I prayed to remain calm, stay focused and give Jordan the strength to hold on.

Two minutes from the hospital, my phone rang. It was Ellena. She was sobbing hysterically. The doctor had left an urgent message on her cell phone moments before reaching me.

"Is he alive?" was all she said not knowing where I was.

"Yes. I just spoke with the doctor, Ellena. He's alive but in critical condition. I'm almost to the hospital. Keep your line open. Don't call anyone. I'll call you the second I know anything."

With that, I hung up, parked and raced into the ER. It was 5:08 a.m. I met immediately with a nurse who took me to the ICU where the doctor was waiting. There was the smell of alcohol, cleaning disinfectants and the sight of IVs running into the patient's arms as nurses seemed to do three jobs at once.

The doctor pulled back a glass door and a curtain to reveal Jordan motionless and unconscious with at least four different machines hooked up to him whirring and clicking. It was a very scary scene. I felt my hands shaking uncontrollably.

The doctor stood at the end of the bed. I stood next to Jordan with my hand on his shoulder.

"Mr. Cassidy, Jordan's condition remains the same. The next 48 to 72 hours will tell us more. His chest x-rays were negative, no broken bones. I'm guessing the bruising was from someone pounding on his chest to revive him. That pumping machine over there is assisting his breathing. He has a collapsed lung. We all need to pray for a miracle," he said.

I immediately closed my eyes and prayed for God to watch over Jordan.

My next thought was to go get my wife. She hated freeway driving. Coupled with this chaos, I knew there would be no way she would be able to drive.

I got the nurse's cell number and told her I would be back and if there were any—I reiterated—*any* changes, for her to call me immediately. As I ran down the hall, I dialed Ellena's number. I was headed back down the 5 to get my wife. That four hour round trip gave me all the time I needed to run several scenarios through my mind, all various ways to keep our family together.

My wife and I spent the next two weeks at Jordan's ICU bedside. We had agreed not to tell anyone, including our daughter. It was strictly on a need to know basis for now. Our daughter, Molly had already faced too many of Jordan's drug problems with his broken promises over the last six years. She would be graduating from high school in a couple months and preparing to begin college. She loved her brother so much but had grown weary of his addiction battle. We needed to protect her too.

The Home Cocoon

This experience was *my* wakeup call. The chance encounter with my professor the year before had already excited me about writing a book on relationships. With the advent of this catastrophe, all of those thoughts about how important everyone around me was, really added fuel to the fire. It got me to thinking about how important my loved ones were, my friends, even my business associates. The content I'd already written from my college paper laid the foundation to talk about trusted meaningful relationships.

Once we learned that Jordan's brain and liver were miraculously intact and unharmed, I knew God's Army of Angels had been protecting him and had always been by his side. Now we needed to begin formulating a game plan. This plan could not be like all the others. We had to do something radical, different, untested. We had to take charge of everything. The rehabilitation facilities, as good as they were, "State of the art," they said, weren't getting the job done. **In my mind, Jordan, my wife and I were the ones not getting the job done.**

As Jordan's vital signs and blood tests got better over those weeks, we got to know an intensive care unit (ICU) nurse well. I will call him Tom. He was running the graveyard shift at the ICU. He asked me one night, "Shawn, what are you going to do? Do you have a plan for Jordan?"

I replied, "We haven't made a final decision but I know it has to be radical. Do you have any suggestions?"

"Yes, I do," he whispered. "But keep this to yourself. I'm not supposed to give out advice."

"I totally understand," I answered leaning into his whisper.

"Shawn, if Jordan was my son and from what I know about his history, and the time I have had with him here, I would take him home. Do **not** take him to another one of those rehabs."

Wow, I was stunned. *No one had ever offered that idea.*

"No Betty Fords, no behavioral institutes, no wilderness camps, no private sobriety group homes; none of that!" He said emphatically.

13

He continued to whisper, "Please, don't get me wrong. So many of those places have done a lot of great work and have saved and changed countless lives but I personally believe that if you and Ellena can commit the time, **just one more time**, I think he'll be ready. Take him home and keep him there. There comes a time..." was how he finished and then gave me a pat on my shoulder as if to say, God's speed.

I couldn't speak for a moment. Tom could see me thinking quietly and perhaps sense my brain racing.

"Shawn. I know your history. You are at the end of your rope. Everyone gets there with this kind of thing. You're not alone. We aren't saints with infinite wisdom and patience. We are just human. That's why there are so many of these young kids in institutions, places they'll never come out of."

"Shawn, you and Ellena take him home and **don't leave him alone 24/7 and find a support program you can institute and follow.**"

I almost broke out in tears as I hugged the big bear of a man thanking him profusely. I called him "Angel Tom" after that. I thought of him as a passionate warrior, a man who was completely committed to helping heal and save people down to his marrow; an unusual man, a real *change agent*.

What was so surreal was that Tom's suggestion to take Jordan home under tight supervision and to seek out some addiction support program was exactly what Ellena had been quietly planning and developing over the past two weeks (unknown to me). Not only was I not aware of her plans, I was stunned when she presented it. Her plan was well researched and meticulous.

Ellena was not only a loving and committed mother, but also a passionate warrior, taking action, bound and determined to help rescue Jordan with a radical disciplined program—she would **NEVER GIVE UP** on our son.

When we all arrived home, Ellena's program, which I whole-heartedly supported, began the minute I opened the front door. Jordan was to have no car access, no phone access and no other form of contact with anyone, including NO INTERNET. The only outside contact would be a weekly two hour counseling session with a local "dry" counselor who was very experienced with teenage drug addiction and his scheduled Alcohol Anonymous meetings. **That was it. Lock down!**

Jordan was allowed two hours a day of television, but only with approved programs, which included News, History Channel, Discovery Channel and some sports.

I won't get into all the details but it is sufficient to say Jordan's typical day included a 6:00 a.m. wake up. He was to make his bed, clean his room, shower and spend two hours a day in **reflection.** In addition, he could read books like the Bible and sobriety and inspirational books, which we provided.

From 7:30 to 8:30 a.m., he had breakfast with Ellena and me and we would socialize and review the plan for the day.

If I had a client to visit, Jordan came with me and kept reading material in the car. When we returned, we worked together in the yard where we got in a good sweat and he got some exercise. He also spent an hour every day on the treadmill. He was allowed to spend two hours a day on his drums, which he loved. At night, he had to sleep with his door open.

In short, he was never out of sight from one or both of us. Ellena escorted him to our required three-night-a-week AA meetings in San Clemente, California and sat through every meeting with him. Though it was a 45-minute drive one-way, we thought it was critical that Jordan be in a new foreign environment. I would add, while there are many good sobriety programs available, I can understand now why Dr. Drew Pinsky, a clinical psychiatrist believes that AA is the best. It's a daily disciplined program, "one day at a time" with no exceptions.

Jordan lived that entire year 100% sober and committed with our support. I will tell you later briefly, how Jordan is today. For now, I am writing this to tell you a little bit more about me and my family and my relationships.

This was a brutal story for several reasons beginning with the obvious—I almost lost my son, which was **without a doubt, the most fearful period of my entire life.**

Secondly, from the time he stepped out of the hospital until the end of that 365 days sequestered in our home, **I** began to grow exponentially in terms of **my gratitude** not only for Jordan, but for every blessing in my life, which not only included my immediate family, but all of my **trusted teams.**

Trusted Team's, as you will soon read, can be any group of two or more people in your family, friendships, community, your workplace, church, school, charity, sports team or whatever group or organization you belong to.

I also learned from Jordan's journey that trusted and meaningful relationships and teams begin with just one person—**you.** From there it grows to include your spouse, son, daughter, brother, mom, dad, sister, grandparent, neighbors, work associates, church members and even your summer softball team. In short, everyone around you—**but it begins with you.**

If you don't invest in your future, don't expect one.
--Jordan Cassidy

Fear is only a "perceived" barrier

I learned so much that year and realized, even after all the many things my father and mother taught me growing up, that I could never escape fear, no matter how much I steeled myself, no matter how often.

For so long, from an intellectual standpoint and from my parents' teachings, I told myself fear was not an option but once again, there it was right in my own living room raising its ugly head when I least expected it (which is generally when it shows up).

As you can see from the title of this book, **fear** is one of the things that keep us all from becoming the best we can possibly be. It is also one of the barriers to trusted and meaningful relationships. However, as with everything else in life, it has its benefits. One of those advantages that I learned during my wakeup call is **fear** reminds us that we can NEVER DO IT ALONE. "Never do what?", you might be asking. Never manage or overcome our deepest fears, never grow to our highest potential, succeed, become fulfilled, contribute, share, give, serve…and we certainly can never learn to do the most important thing we are here on planet earth for, LOVE.

Love is the ultimate. You cannot give it if you don't have someone, some group, and some passion to share it with. Likewise, success, fulfillment, growth, service, do **not** occur in a vacuum.

Thus began my journey to writing this book. First, there was the serendipitous meeting with an old professor, then there was **reflection** on my part, then there were notes piling up on my desk, then WHAM! like a Nolan Ryan 100 m.p.h. fastball hit me in the face—my son was dying, maybe in the next five minutes and I was a hundred miles away. However, 100 miles physically was nothing compared to the distance of the emotional, spiritual and intellectual journey I was about to take—the journey to fully understanding the importance of trusted relationships and how they all begin with just one step.

Take the journey with me now as I tell you my story…

Think about this for a moment before I continue…

No matter how long or how short your life is, you **only** get…

86,400 seconds each day.

If you are like most of us, you **sleep away** about **28,000** of those seconds.

Only

58,400 seconds left.

The clock is **TICKING…**

Now, if you take away time for…

Arguing with your spouse about some trivial thing you wish you'd never brought up,

worrying about bills,

regretting something in your past, you can't do anything about,

being afraid of something that might happen tomorrow (but often doesn't),

spending too much time being "social" online,

criticizing or judging other people...

I'm guessing, based on the average person's life, you now have about...

14,000 seconds left in your day if you're lucky. That isn't much.

The clock is ticking...

Perhaps that will give you pause to think. How precious is time? Only you can answer that for yourself, but if you asked a 90-year old man or woman that question, you would almost certainly get a different answer. Ask the disaster survivor who lived through a tsunami, or an injured combat vet who narrowly escaped death, or that guy down the block who had quadruple bypass surgery last month and lived to tell you about it, or God forbid (and forgive me for even bringing it up), the couple who just lost their child who they hadn't talked to in a month.

None of us has enough time to waste a second in this life but sadly, **many of us are experts at it.** If you could use that 14,000 seconds tomorrow that you were going to lose, you would have more than…

FOUR EXTRA HOURS every day to…
grow, to love, to help someone, to inspire a child, to reflect on this miracle that is life….

I think you get the point.

Now, here is someone who had nothing BUT time on his hands. In fact, he spent 27 years of his life in prison—the apartheid activist, Nelson Mandela. When he was finally released, was later interviewed and asked how he survived he told the reporter he never felt imprisoned, that in fact, he felt complete freedom, **freedom of the mind was more important** than freedom of the body.

Mandela was not comfortable by any means, but he carried no fears, no worries, and no animosities. He had learned to come to a place of unequivocal peace and freedom no matter where he was because he had relinquished all fear of anything. No matter what they did to him, they couldn't stop him from thinking. His mind was a vast universe of potential positive thoughts.

I learned that courage was not the absence of fear, but the triumph over it. The brave man is not he who does not feel afraid, but he who conquers that fear.

--Nelson Mandela

Thoughts to remember from
Chapter One: State of the Art

-The title of this book: **The secrets to growth, fulfillment and success through trusted and meaningful relationships**

- **Our *connected* world… is actually becoming more and more
DISCONNECTED.**

- We buy into these ***transactions*** because no one wants to be lonely. Nobody wants to feel like he is on the outside looking in

- the world's need for intelligent, clear, loving, **values-based relationships** is greater now than ever before in history!

-What will your wakeup call be? Have you received yours yet?

- **NEVER GIVE UP**

- **Trusted Teams** can be any group of **two** or more people in your family, friendships, community, your workplace, church, school, charity, sports team or whatever group or organization you belong to.

- Fear cannot be a barrier

-We can never do it ALONE

-What will you do with your **FOUR EXTRA HOURS TODAY?**

NOTES:

I encourage you to write your thoughts in this space. Make note of some action items you want to remember. This will fire up your Head, Heart and Gut as you begin the H$_2$G Revolution.

Chapter Two
The Trusted Relationship

Trust is its own reward.

How important are trusted and meaningful relationships in our lives? For me, *my greatest opportunities both personal and business successes since childhood were all made possible by understanding and building trusted relationships.*

Some people refer to trusted relationships as "teamwork," and a team effort is always important and in fact, is a critical part of the **H₂G Revolution.** However, building trusted relationships goes much deeper than that. My goal is to introduce a new way to know, define and understand "team."

Since the days when I began my own journey and started writing this book, I questioned over 300 business executives, CEO's, parents, high school and college students, teachers, physicians, senior citizens, regular people from all occupations. I asked each an open-ended question: *How important are meaningful and trusted relationships in your life?*

96% of the respondents provided the same one word answer: **"Everything!"**

That did not come as a surprise to me. Without these trusted and meaningful relationships, they said their lives would be "empty, sad, lonely, disconnected, discontented, or unfulfilled."

More concerning to me though is what I touched on in the introduction–**in our new fast-paced "connected" technology driven world, we are not making the time to invest and nurture these kinds of relationships.** We know they really matter and make a difference in our lives and yet when asked why, most of those same individuals polled agreed that it isn't the fault of technology. They felt it was our own fascination, obsession, distraction, and addiction to the "toys of technology" and information access, or the harried, chaotic manner in which we allow ourselves to fall prey to, the **chaos of our own making.**

Why do you suppose so many people are fascinated with these transactions of technology, or allow their lives to become so busy or frenetic?

"Technology time" has ironically taken away real time from our relationships that we know mean everything. Add to this, the time stolen from being unnecessarily rushed, stressed and overworked and many of us feel ultimately that NOTHING CAN WAIT.

So many distractions seem to muscle their way into our important relationships. Everything yells at us, "I'm important. Respond to me first. Read my blog. See my last Facebook posting." Answer my phone call.

How do we fix this when so many people don't really want to and don't realize the impact on their relationships? How do we change and prioritize the things that really matter? We all get it or think we do! We all *say* we need and want more valuable and committed relationships. We want to be part of reliable and trusted teams in order to realize growth and happiness.

If we are becoming too comfortable and complacent with this new "reality," are we resigning and giving up on investing in the relationships that really matter?

Is it like being overweight and out of shape? For many, we know we are overweight and should begin that diet immediately. We also know that the exercise would pay huge health benefits and we'd live longer to enjoy our families and friends. We know we should carve out a consistent daily program and stick to it. **How many of us do it?**

From January 1-15th, the entire country is on a two week disciplined diet and exercise program, our New Year's resolutions! Then, slowly but surely our **resolve** becomes **dissolve,** not so much because we are quitters, but because all of those "important" things in our lives begin to crowd in again. Sadly, those important things aren't always working on our trusted relationships or teams, or helping us to learn, grow and find fulfillment.

However, unlike our New Year's resolutions, the solution to building and nurturing our meaningful relationships does not come with a patented workout program or diet plan. There are no Cliff Notes or study guides to building meaningful relationships, no secret organic food supplements, no miracle liquid drink or special vitamins that will guarantee results—but like our "resolutions," there **ARE** exercises.

Toward the end of this book, I will present you with a plan I call, **H₂G,** which stands for **Head**, **Heart** and **Gut** and I will give you the **H₂G** formula for developing and using these three core elements of who you are. They are presented in an easy to follow daily journey of discovery and a growth you never thought possible. **It will be a journey you will not take alone and I promise you tangible results will start the day you begin.**

Building meaningful relationships is a transformational healthy mindset and lifestyle that takes consistent real work on a daily disciplined plan. It means adopting and embracing a passion to succeed every day.

Ever since Jordan's near death, I find myself asking the question: Isn't it really all about the quality of our relationships at the end of the day that really matters? If your answer is yes, then ask yourself:

Throughout my life, today and in my final days on this earth, how strong and meaningful will my family, business, social and spiritual relationships be?

If you found out in the next hour or tomorrow that someone you loved dearly all your life was dying, how would you change your relationship with him or her and as important, how would you change **all** of your relationships with your fellow human beings? Would you be filled with regret or would you know in your heart that you gave everything you could?

EVERYTHING!

Where are you in your relationships? Are you pro-active and committed to honestly working to understand, nurture and grow them? Are you committed to encourage, inspire and help a family, friend or work team member who may be discouraged, depressed or even battling alcohol or drug addiction? **Or,** are you complacent and comfortable just getting through another boring or hectic day, making minimal investments and sitting on the sidelines just to say or hope a relationship exists?

Are you battling your own **fears**? We all have them. Do you have fears that have you caged in your own prison or hiding behind your computer screen, keeping you from truly living a happy and fulfilled life? Are you going through life aimlessly neglecting and avoiding what you know you should do or really want to do constantly making excuses that you just don't have enough time in your crazy day to tackle it? You'll start on it "sometime" next week; that sometime, that **never** comes.

We all set daily **priorities** in life. However, priorities are not necessarily positive and don't always contribute to growth.

Sadly, sometimes, priorities are just getting through the day.

Unfortunately, all too often, in both our personal and business world, it's not until we are served with a "crisis notification" that we truly realize and appreciate the importance of living and growing our relationships.

Every one of us will inevitably receive a summons or be confronted with the challenging or even devastating "wake-up" call to a crisis in our lifetime. That can be a permanent disability, life threatening health issue, sudden loss of a loved one—there are many and most of the time, they come as surprises. So, when the summons arrives, can we survive the crisis and chaos or will we become crippled and paralyzed with negative emotions and resigned to living a less fulfilling and meaningful life? Remember, fear is a "perceived" barrier, but

FEAR can be a powerful ally too! **In addition, I will show you how as you continue your journey.**

The strength and foundation of our valued relationships, or the ones we will seek to build, will determine how well we address and cope with all of our challenges. The strength of these relationships will also be the catalyst to your growth, success and happiness. The POWER of these meaningful relationships will change your world, the world of your friends, family and associates and eventually (and I truly believe this with all my heart)...the entire world. **(I know that's a lot to promise, but stick with me.)**

How often have we personally lived the experience or heard the story: *Without the help or support of that special someone or that special group in my life, I couldn't have made it or, thank God I got a second chance or it would have been all over?*

At some point, we will all realize that we just cannot do it alone.

How many family, friends, or work colleagues do you know right now who are masking or running from their fears, only to be living unsatisfied and unfulfilled lives?

In the case with my son, he always reminds me that he found the courage to overcome addiction and chose sobriety (his particular fear), only because all the support was there. We never gave up on him and every real, caring "team member" in his world has been a difference maker in continuing his sobriety. His strong belief and relationship with his all-powerful and knowing God (his higher power), daily self-discipline, his AA family, our strong family relationship and the pure joy and fulfillment he gets from his job as a mechanic and being part of a professional team, are his keys to growth and sobriety.

His case is no exception.

Too often, our fears or ego causes us to remain distant and truly disconnected with family, friends, support groups and professionals who could really help us.

Though it is only one issue in a host of problems, it is a huge one: the tragedy of teenage drug and alcohol abuse across America is an absolute epidemic that is out of control. Too many parents want to quietly ignore the problem and justify and rationalize it as just a teenage phase their child is going through. Some parents are battling their own addiction issues. Others, facing reality, are beside themselves, living the daily nightmare of an uncontrollable drug addicted son or daughter, desperately searching for help and the right answers.

Without our good health and meaningful relationships in life, we are treading in treacherous waters. The sooner we can take the first step to realize that our mental, physical and emotional health, coupled with all our desires to have meaningful relationships is **Everything** – the sooner the **H₂G Revolution** will begin.

Okay, enough about the problems.
How about some solutions?

The beginnings of my research in college remain the same today. My desire to find the steps that were involved in quality relationships led me to the analogy of a ladder. I call it simply, **The Trusted Relationship Ladder: 7 Steps to Understanding and Building the Trusted Relationship.** It may look like a staircase as well and that's ok. Either way, you start at the bottom and begin to climb…

> **Unconditional Trust**
> **Trust**
> **Respect**
> **Opportunity**
> **Competency**
> **Understanding**
> **LIKEABILITY**

Like a ladder or any climb, the first step is the easiest and the closest to where you are at the moment and so I will begin with the first rung, LIKEABILITY, and work up to the pinnacle…UNCONDITIONAL TRUST.

When we are introduced to others for the first time, we all tend to make a positive or negative impression. Rarely is it ever neutral because we are inquisitive, biased, judging creatures. (Notice that I said, "make" an impression and not "give" one.)

The reason is that for the most part, **we are in charge** of leaving every individual we meet with the impression we choose to impart, whether we were cognizant of it or not.

Many times, this first impression and assessment whether accurate or not, is the determining factor in the possible development of a relationship.

"You never get a second chance to make a first impression."

-Anon

If people have a good impression of someone, it is common for one to be curious about that person and want to know more about him or her. **During that first impression, the first step of exploring and building the relationship is taken, knowingly or not.**

On the other hand, we have all heard experienced or witnessed those encounters where someone was a turn off or at best so bland as to be forgotten in moments. If that person was a turn off, it might have been because they were self-involved (the most common annoyance), distant, aggressive—you can fill in the blank. After that first encounter, it is possible that person remains an acquaintance, neighbor or a recognized "face", but not a relationship, not someone you would want on your team.

With this caveat though, I would add, never say never. We have all experienced "second chance" encounters where perceptions change.

It's hard sometimes when we meet people for the first time to not over judge or to immediately assess who they really are. It's important that we truly try to be open-minded and fair. There are many out there today, spouses, partners, work colleagues, who would tell you their very first impression with their NOW trusted team member was actually weak or marginal at best and there was likely no future in them ever believing a trusted relationship could materialize.

                        Unconditional Trust
                        Trust
                    Respect
                Opportunity
            Competency
        UNDERSTANDING
...Likeability

When people leave your presence with a positive impression, it is probable that "likeability" was an important factor. If the first impression was a pleasant, enjoyable and a memorable experience, the door was probably open for the next step, or what I call, *personal profile understanding.*

You could call this a crossroads where connections are discovered and shared. It is where we begin the journey of learning all about another person's background, upbringing, parents, family, schooling, values, and culture, religion, work and life experiences. It's truly amazing how much we can really learn about someone when the initial likeability factor is high.

UNDERSTANDING.

People like openly sharing with others they feel comfortable with.

Often times, early in the relationship, we learn far more than we could have imagined. Sometimes, the emerging relationship may be over because certain information was revealed that we just can't feel comfortable moving ahead with in a trusted relationship. Understanding and discovering another person's *personal profile* is fundamental and necessary to building a trusted relationship.

If you can't begin to *know* and understand a person, one can never expect anything more than a shallow and superficial connection, perhaps filled with nothing but the occasional *transaction* and not the real building blocks of human development that are needed to grow a trusted relationship.

Think how true this really is. So many people after a favorable first personal or business introduction and impression, are *too* ready to have people trust them. Many of us are so trusting and big hearted that we really want to fast track the relationship building process, immediately after that outstanding first impression. However, most of us also know, particularly after an unfortunate hard lesson that real relationship development rarely works that way. It takes actual invested time to know a person.

There is an important reason why meaningful and trusted relationships take time to understand and build. It's not unlike growing a plant; it's a process. It takes work, effort, care and commitment to help those seeds to push through the ground, maintain the tender shoots and leaves, and then continue to grow it into a thriving plant. Even then, the work isn't complete, it never is, there is always maintenance— fertilizer, pruning, watering and even kind words. **Understanding.**

Unconditional Trust
Trust
Respect
Opportunity
COMPETENCY
Understanding
...Likeability

The third of the seven steps to trusted relationships is core **competency**. We all admire those who are bright and intelligent, those who have the best academic or vocational schooling, impeccable credentials, proven work experiences and impressive performance records.

We all want the best physician, financial advisor, mechanic, hair stylist, personal trainer or boss. It's important and necessary that the core competency components of **knowledge, integrity, expertise, experience, commitment, and results** not only be learned, acquired and maintained, but also demonstrated! Core **competency** is critical in building trust.

You can be as smart as Albert Einstein, but if you cannot effectively convey, articulate, and demonstrate your core competency knowledge, value and skill set, your **real** value will not be fully understood; it won't be recognized and appreciated. How many bright people are stuck or lost because they cannot effectively express their talents or work well with people? Too many to count.

Everyone likes to say and know that they are working with, for, or have been hired by the best. Being committed and being recognized as the "best of the best," on your team is one of the most powerful, influential and meaningful elements in building trust and opening the doors for opportunity in your relationships. **Competency.**

Unconditional Trust

Trust

Respect

OPPORTUNITY

Competency

Understanding

...Likeability

Stepping up the ladder of the attributes that comprise a trusted relationship is **opportunity.**

If building a relationship is a test (as it often is in both our personal and business lives) then assuming you employ the first three attributes, at some point, you will be presented or awarded an opportunity. (This ladder of course, also applies to your family, friends and other social environments, but underneath it all, it's still a test. The opportunity could be a special assignment, a new job, a service contract, a real estate listing, a new relationship, or a myriad of other things.)

Three or four outcomes will take place after you've accepted an opportunity. **The first** might be outright success—you hit it out of the park by exceeding expectations with an outstanding performance.

The second outcome could be that you end up performing as expected but you have done nothing outstanding or memorable. At that point, you stay in the game and are likely given another opportunity to see what you can do.

The third possibility would be that you fail, which could have been through circumstances beyond your control, a team colleague dropped the ball, an equipment failure, or a host of other unfortunate conditions or excuses. The future of the relationship may be over depending on the fall out damage realized.

The last possible outcome is that you will be given a second chance, another opportunity. People can be very understanding and forgiving, particularly when someone is forthright and honest with his or her failure. Also if this person, boss, teacher or mentor genuinely liked you, understood you, and believed in your abilities, he or she may likely give you that special second chance opportunity to redeem and improve your "performance" so that your relationship can have the opportunity to continue building and going forward.

This holds true in the personal side of our relationships as well. We are all human and we have all made our share of questionable, poor judgments or just down right stupid mistakes in our relationships. I like to remind myself, and I have been humbled along the way, that I think we all live in personal fragile glass houses.

While the courting and honeymoon opportunities are often home runs with experiences and memories that last a lifetime, all relationships are nearly continually tested. It takes honest self-awareness, effective communication, empathy, compassion, generosity, gratitude, commitment, faith and that special ingredient of forgiveness, to understand and to continue to grow our relationships. **Opportunity.**

Unconditional Trust
Trust
RESPECT
Opportunity
Competency
Understanding
...Likeability

The next critical rung on the ladder, and it's a big step, is **respect.** People can *like* you, *understand* you; know you have loads of talent (competency) and ability. However, if they do not *respect* you, that relationship will hit a serious roadblock or potential dead-end…

Respect is not a birthright. Unfortunately, too many people think it is and even demand it as if they were entitled for no particular reason other than their own egos or some arbitrary rank or title.

Respect must be earned. When it is, we are all proud and pleased to openly give it or receive it when rightfully earned. It builds loyalty and is an absolute critical and necessary building block to establishing trust. Loyalty in turn builds trust. It can never be a self-described entitlement. We all know nothing is worse than to see someone being promoted or given a position or title in an organization who is not respected, or the parent, coach, colleague or boss, who demands respect, but hasn't earned it. Few things rival this nearly universal distaste.

Reaching trust is what everyone would hope to achieve in a strong business or personal relationship. It embraces and validates all the critical and necessary components to achieve this coveted status: **likability, understanding, competency, opportunity, respect and trust.**

When it comes to trust: **integrity, accountability, commitment, and confidentiality** are all special and critical ingredients. The established relationship of trust takes time to build and can never be expected to happen overnight.

However, even with years of building and maintaining a trusted relationship, it can still be lost forever in the blink of an eye if ever violated. **One of the most difficult tasks in life is to regain trust. It is almost like trying to un-ring the bell.**

Trust not only fuels and energizes personal and business relationships, but is necessary if anyone or any company is going to be truly successful over time. Trust is the "everything" in relationships as discussed earlier **when 96 % of everyone** polled said that trusted and meaningful relationships are everything. Without it, at best, you have uncertainty and suspicion and at worst, fear and distrust. Distrust is extremely contagious, infectious, and lethal to every personal and business relationship.

It doesn't happen overnight as educator and author Dr. Stephan R. Covey clearly conveys, "Trust is the highest of human motivations. It brings out the very best in people. But, it takes time and patience."

Every high performing and successful company values, embraces and seeks to build trust within their ranks and with their customers every single day of their existence.

Relationship coach Carl S. Avery, sums up trust when he writes,

"Trust enables you to put your deepest feelings and fears in the palm of your partner's hands, knowing they will be **handled** with care".

When we read and learn that 50% of employees of a given company don't have trust in their senior management and one in every two marriages ends in divorce in the U.S., it's easy to understand why trust is so important.

The question is how do we build and acquire this sacred virtue? More on that later with a special lifestyle formula, The H_2G Revolution. **Trust.**

We have arrived at the uppermost rung on the relationship ladder. **UNCONDTIONAL TRUST** is one that in many cases will never be reached by most of us. However, there *is* a very small group of people that *will* reach and experience this extraordinary level of trust in their lifetimes.

UNCONDITIONAL TRUST
Trust
Respect
Opportunity
Competency
Understanding
...Likeability

Unconditional trust is often only realized after it has been experienced as in giving one's life for another. This has been documented repeatedly in special family experiences, wars, combat missions with special teams and natural civilian disasters.

Unconditional trust is extraordinarily rare. **It means letting go.** There are **no** conditions, no if's, maybe's or let me think about that, can we talk about it tomorrow, I'll get back to you on that, no biases of any kind.

Unconditional trust is the pinnacle; no questions asked, no excuses given, just pure love and action. It is gained only through time, effort, love and the climbing of the Trusted Relationship Ladder. It is not difficult at that stage because there is no forethought needed. It simply IS.

You only receive it through a concerted, loving, long effort, the end of which is complete release, a giving in to another person outside yourself.

Unconditional trust is the complete **absence of EGO.** It is thinking of someone, some group or team more than you. It is not easy to achieve and if it is ever broken, it can NEVER be rebuilt.

Oddly, unconditional trust is not about others so much as it is about you. It is your opportunity to grow, to learn, to love and be loved unconditionally with no rules, regulations, prior infractions. It's your OPPORTUNITY to change you.

When the famous former heavyweight boxing champion, Mike Tyson, was asked on the 60 Minutes television program recently, what turned his life around, what made him change, he replied (and I'm paraphrasing here),

"I killed my EGO. I kill my ego every day. I changed because there was something higher and more important than me—my wife and my children, things I love unconditionally. Compared to that, I was alone. I was small and insignificant."

Thoughts to remember for
Chapter Two: Trusted Relationships

- *How important are meaningful and trusted relationships in your life?* **96%** of the respondents to my question provided the same one word answer: **"Everything!"**

- **H₂G** stands for Head, Heart and Gut.

- **At some point, we will all realize that we just cannot do it alone.**

- Do you have fears that have you caged in your own prison or hiding behind your computer screen, keeping you from truly living a happy and fulfilled life?

- FEAR can be a powerful ally too!

-The 7-step ladder…

<u>**UNCONDITIONAL TRUST**</u>
Trust
Respect
Opportunity
Competency
Understanding
…Likeability

- Even with years of building and maintaining a trusted relationship, it can still be lost forever in the blink of an eye if ever violated. **One of the most difficult tasks in life is to regain trust. It is almost like trying to un-ring the bell.**

NOTES:

I encourage you to write your thoughts in this space. Make note of some action items you want to remember. This will fire up your Head, Heart and Gut as you begin the H_2G Revolution.

Chapter Three
The Power of Teams

Everything we've been talking about concerning relationships start with one more than ME. In short—**teams**.

I know that the word "teamwork" is overused and a lot of you might be growing numb to it, but maybe there is a reason we hear it so often.

Not all relationships are trusted and meaningful. However, many "groups" that you belong to have the potential to become teams and within those teams, you can develop trusted and meaningful relationships.

You have already read about the 7 rungs on the Trusted Relationship Ladder…

UNCONDITIONAL TRUST
Trust
Respect
Opportunity
Competency
Understanding
…Likeability

These are the steps to helping you understand and develop TRUSTED and MEANINGFUL RELATIONSHIPS. These are the **ACTION** steps we all need to learn and become proficient with in order to grow yourself and your team.

What is a **TEAM** and why are they so important?
A team is **two or more people.**

In our social world, potential teams that we can join surround us—our workplace, your children's school, our college sports teams, a place of worship, a charity, and the list is practically endless. The point is we don't have any excuses to think that we are alone. In fact, in the spiritual world, if you are a believer in a higher power, YOU ARE NEVER ALONE. You have **that** team member that never leaves your side and is available to you 24/7, 365 days a year or...

86,400 seconds a day...

Without trusted and meaningful relationships, it is very difficult to grow, find peace, become prosperous or be fulfilled completely.

It takes two or more to tango. **There are no savings accounts for love.** You can't stockpile it or hoard it. There is no value in it until it is shared. Unconditional trust involves surrender.

I will be talking about FEAR a lot in this book and **THE POWER OF TEAMS** and why we cannot do it all alone.

However, before I jump more into fear, I would like to introduce you to what I call, "Team Cassidy." This is where the power of teams all started for me. This is where my letting go began. It will introduce you to my family and how we developed into a phenomenal trusted team.

Coming together is a beginning. Keeping together is progress. Working together is success.

-- Henry Ford

Team Cassidy

In the Cassidy home, all "team members" five years of age and older, participated in daily household chores (I have six siblings.)

Dad posted a matrix listing all seven kids: Brenda, Belinda, Shawn, Ann, Colleen, Kathy and Shane (born within nine years from 1956 through 1965).

On Dad's matrix all our individual or team daily and weekly tasks and chores were clearly listed. A new list was posted every two weeks in the kitchen. The list would contain **every** job or task that one could imagine and more. One of the toughest and most dreaded weekly chores was the bathroom grout cleaning detail, which had to be performed with an old toothbrush. We used a bathroom tile cleaner and bleach to clean the shower and floor tile grout to ensure no dirt, bacteria or mold build-up ever appeared in the Cassidy's household.

The good news was that there were always two team members assigned to this chore. It only took us one time to learn that we had better wear the provided rubber gloves to save our fingers and skin.

The itemized kitchen chore list would look like this: wash, dry, put away dishes,

wipe/clean counter tops,
clean base boards,
sweep/clean floor,
trash out,
refrigerator cleaned with an additional once a week, complete interior "clean-out" including all jar/bottle lids & tops,
sink cleaned,
cabinets cleaned,
all cooking utensils organized,
stove/oven cleaned,
walls cleaned.

Every one of us kids was responsible for keeping his or her room tidy; beds made, clothes picked up, closets clean and organized and Lord save you if you ever left a light on or radio playing if you were not in the room—wasting electricity was not a good thing. Dad would always say that he didn't want to receive a Christmas card from the utility company thanking the Cassidy's for record electric or water usage.

My father created and assigned a total of 52 regular (daily or weekly) household chores. With nine in our household, we always had a three-ring work circus going from washing clothes, vacuuming, and just keeping the "fort" organized. While Mom's name wasn't on the list, she did more work than all of us combined. Her life was constantly helping each of us with chores, schoolwork, and life's every day challenges.

What a teacher my mother was. The greatest gift she had was her **unconditional love** and positive attitude that only a Mother Theresa type could match. In all my years, I have never met a person with a more positive, loving and inspirational attitude, not only with her children, but also with all those she touched.

After raising seven kids, my mother opened her own "Nana & Papa" home child day care operation. For the next 10 years after we were raised, she nurtured and loved countless infants and toddlers while my dad played the supporting role as "Papa", helped Mom on a daily basis with the four to five infants they were caring for Monday through Friday.

My mother also went on to become a national childcare advocate for the professional day development and licensing industry serving as Vice President for the National Association For Family Child Care (NAFCC).

She was completely giving into supporting great childrens' causes. As far back as I can remember she walked the beaches with my Dad at sunset in California and Virginia to collect thousands of seashells from which she made beautiful ornaments and wreaths for sale. All proceeds were donated to the St Jude's Children's Research Hospital.

My mother passed away on June 4, 2003, just two months after being diagnosed with cancer. Before coming home to the loving support of her family and a professional hospice caregiver in her final weeks, she **never stopped** inspiring and serving. The difference she made in so many lives at the hospital was unbelievable and will never be forgotten. I didn't learn this until the day of Mom's memorial service when nurses came up to me to express their gratitude for her. So many told me that they had never met and encountered a more loving, caring woman than my Mom.

Many asked me what it was like growing up with a mother like her.

"Pure love and always giving," was my reply. The most meaningful impact from all the nurses was to learn that they all took time off from work to attend Mom's funeral to celebrate her life. I also learned that they had to coordinate staffing with two area hospitals in order to get enough outside help to cover all the nurses that attended at Mom's service.

After that service, perhaps the most meaningful experience for me was meeting a young nurse's aide named Keri who came up to tell me, "Your mother inspired me every day! I'm now attending school at night studying for my Registered Nurse certification and state nursing license."

She continued, "Your mother gave me the confidence and courage to go for it! I could not have done this without her encouragement!

"Your mother told me the nursing industry needed special people like me and that I could make a real difference in serving people."

Though a great blessing to that young woman, that was no surprise to me. Mom **lived** and **demonstrated** a phenomenal level of loving, caring and giving every day of her life. She also always encouraged, inspired and taught everyone to follow his/her own passion and purpose in life right up to her last remaining hours on earth.

This is the remarkable end to that story. On the day she **knew** she was going to leave us, she requested that each one of us (family) come by her bedside for a one on one special moment together. She shared a special loving message with each one of her seven children before spending her final hours with my father. Sitting in the recliner chair that night, I heard her recite her love story with Dad, her final goodbyes and a kiss before she closed her eyes and began her journey to heaven. They shared three incredible final hours together—what a blessing. Talk about the seconds ticking.

From the first time they met, to all the military moves, to the special life she shared with my Dad and her seven children and 13 grandchildren, hers was an unbelievable and unforgettable spiritual life experience that I wish everyone could witness or experience with their parent or loved one.

Mom had no regrets. She truly lived a passionate, happy and totally fulfilled life.

She epitomized UNCONDITIONAL LOVE and knew more than anyone I've ever known what a TRUSTED, MEANINGFUL RELATIONSHIP was all about.

The Parenting Team

In my eyes, the Cassidy team ended up having the perfect parent balance. My father was the disciplined "teacher," often with tough love. He was a proud hard charging career U.S. Marine officer and a caring father who ran a tight or near perfect schedule, but always worked to make it fun!

Mom was the most loving and inspiring mother that anyone could ever dream of having. She was there 24-7 for us, including the four years when Dad was absent and deployed during his combat tours in Vietnam.

Every day, our parents taught us all the importance of family, love, determination, persistence, work ethic, accountability, effective communication, gratitude, competition, excellence, faith, forgiveness, empathy, tolerance, and of course, TEAM. To have one role model parent in life is special, but to have two, is rare and a pure blessing that my brother, my sisters and I will forever be grateful for.

NBA star basketball player, Michael Jordan summed it up best when he wrote about a common belief we both share,

"My heroes are and were my parents. I can't see having anyone else as my heroes".

A powerful team in action
The Cassidy Team Inspection

It started with our nightly dinner gathering, which was always prepared and served by Mom at 5:30 p.m. If you arrived five minutes late, without having been at a school sport practice/game or some other acceptable activity, you were not "invited" to the dinner table. We would hang out in our rooms until the dinner hour ended at 6:30 p.m. We didn't perceive this as any harsh punishment, it was just the rule. However, after dinner, we were invited down to join in with the clean up or the kitchen detail.

Dad made sure everyone had an assigned chore in the kitchen. During dinner, if we'd made it promptly, we would go around the table and each child would share his/her school day experience. We would then all participate in an open family discussion about national politics and current events. That was always an exciting experience because Dad was a strong Barry Goldwater conservative and Mom was a strong JFK liberal. Both articulated their political views and always gave us a keen understanding and appreciation for a balanced political perspective as well as a balanced perspective in all things without fighting!

Mom and Dad expected all the kids to be well versed and "up to speed" on current national affairs.

One memorable night I will never forget, Dad taught us all the true meaning of TEAM. I was nine years old and in the fourth grade. We were living in military officer housing. Dad was stationed at the Camp Pendleton Marine base (north of San Diego) and was ready for his third combat deployment to Vietnam.

That particular evening after completing our kitchen detail, we went into the living room to let Dad know we were ready for "inspection". From 6:30 p.m.-7:00 p.m., Dad would always watch the CBS Evening News with Walter Cronkite, "The Most Trusted Man in America," according to a Gallup poll at the time.

He would often enjoy his evening news with his favorite after dinner dessert, which included a glass of wine with some Ritz crackers, Swiss cheese and horseradish.

"Are you sure you're ready?" was Dad's response.

"Yes, we are," we would all chime in.

When my father walked in, we were all lined up. He looked around, eyeing the floor, counter tops and sink. He opened the silverware drawer and pulled out a spoon buried in the rubber utensil dividers. Holding the spoon up over his head under the sink light, he would scrutinize it just as if he were inspecting a company of Marines.

He would look at that spoon from three different angles, all part of the drama, as if he were looking for a mirror image with an exaggerated contorted look on his face. This evening, there was no food on the spoon (there rarely was) but there were some visible residue hard water spots; it wasn't looking too good for our kitchen detail team.

Dad immediately plugged the sink with the stopper, turned on the hot water and dropped the spoon in the steaming hot water. He then reached under the sink to grab the liquid soap and a gallon jug of bleach, squirting a quick shot of soap in the sink and then pouring a half cup of bleach into the water. He then very calmly pulled out the whole silverware drawer from the cabinet frame and flipped the drawer full of silverware—over 60 knives, forks and spoons, into the sink.

He turned around, seeing our chagrined faces and in a very low and direct voice, making eye contact with each of us said, "Now, let me know when you are ready for inspection!"

Without a further word, he headed back to his favorite recliner to watch the end of the news.

As soon as he was out of earshot, the finger pointing and verbal blaming began: who was responsible, who was to blame for the "dirty" spoon, but we immediately all pitched in and started over. Twenty minutes later, after double-checking the entire kitchen, we called Dad in for our re-inspection.

This time he did not need to ask us if we were ready. He walked in and quickly asked who cleaned the counters. Colleen raised her hand, "I did," she said.

"Now, that's a job well done. Outstanding," he said.

He then turned to everyone without ever opening the silverware drawer and asked, "Now, what did we learn on this kitchen detail tonight"?

Everyone was silent as he began a familiar refrain.

"We are all responsible and accountable to everyone on the team! We succeed and fail as a team. We can't expect to be perfect all the time and we need to learn and grow from our mistakes and failures. When given a job to do, we need to do it RIGHT the FIRST time, ALL the time.

"Nothing will be done half ass and there will be no short cuts! In my world and in the outside world, you often don't get a second chance to get it right and in some cases, we lose men when we don't do it right!"

He was obviously referring to his active duty as a Marine when he said, "We lost way too many. So, going forward, let's get it right the first time, all the time! Good job, now, get out of here," which was always said with a big smile.

This foundational TEAM life lesson has always stayed with me and has always given me a strong and clear understanding of the importance and purpose of TEAMwork and being responsible and accountable as a Team member in my personal and business life. Striving to give your best, learning and growing from setbacks and failures as a TEAM, develops lasting and trusting relationships.

Even with that as my guiding principle, later in life, I found myself making a huge financial mistake, a mistake that I made as a sober, intelligent adult. I experienced deep soul searching and regret. However, with the resolution of it all, I came out a stronger person and a stronger team player. That trusted and meaningful relationship I shared with my family enabled me to grow and to know that we all make mistakes and we all fail and yet, many of us see those not as stop signs, but as lessons.

Unfortunately, I had to learn **that** lesson twice—first as a youngster and later as an adult. It was all about two things: first, being honest and second, **being responsible and accountable for all my actions.** That was at the core of my growth and so I learned that it was an opportunity. After my initial regret and sorrow over my abysmal choice, I became driven. All of that negative experience made me a far more positive individual.

In thinking about my early college paper, writing this book and about that mistake, **I realized many of us have been taught to view mistakes as failures so we recoil and crawl under the "fear blanket" afraid that we'll do it again.** Making mistakes in a lot of our culture is the boogieman, the scarlet letter, a sign of weakness, stupidity or bad judgment when in fact**, it's not a mistake to fail; it's a mistake not to learn and to try again.**

We NEED to make mistakes otherwise we aren't really trying. We cannot dream that we are going to reach for the moon and do it without some stumbles. Nothing is perfect.

Most of the incredible entrepreneurs like Richard Branson were at their most courageous when they were faced with the possibility of making the wrong or a bad choice. The key for successful people is to view **fears as opportunities**, not roadblocks.

I am so grateful for learning those lessons and having the backup of my most trusted and meaningful team—my family. We need to learn that making mistakes can be a badge of courage. We need to understand that NO ONE does it alone or does it to perfection, especially the first time. Mistakes are part of our growth.

My mother and father knew their **team parent** priorities in life were much more than as providers of shelter, food and protection. They were both committed and passionate full-time teachers and life role models who taught us it was all about Team. My Dad's favorite words of wisdom were, "If you all commit 100% to serving the Team, success will be your outcome in the end."

My mother would always remind us that a truly fulfilled life was ALL about **living, loving, learning** and **making a difference**, particularly in a child's life.

Second Chance

Second chance is another power team story. I bring it up because I believe it demonstrates how your team can make all the difference in your challenges and fears.

In 1976, my family moved to Virginia Beach, Virginia where I would finish my last two years of high school at First Colonial. This was our sixth family move growing up, not uncommon for a military family. First California, Missouri and then Virginia.

Meeting new classmates, making new friends and joining new sports teams is not always "easy duty" for any child and military transplants are no exception.

Over those years and moves, I learned to embrace the same battle cry our U.S. Marines and other military branches are trained to live by and practice every day:

IMPROVISE,

ADAPT, and

OVERCOME...a good philosophy for anyone.

In the spring of my junior year, with one year of making friends and playing in school sports, I decided I was going to run for Student Body President for my coming senior year.

Even though I was the new kid on the block, I felt confident that I could win and had the backing of many different groups. I was President of my 9th-10th grade class at my previous high school in Missouri and I was ready to jump in again. I devoted myself to a three-week campaign that I poured my heart, soul and body into. When the votes were counted, out of over 2,000 ballots, I lost by 18 votes.

It was so close there was an automatic recount. I waited in the school cafeteria barely able to breathe. After waiting what seemed an eternity, my sister Ann, one year younger and my unofficial campaign manager, broke the bad news. I was devastated. It was difficult to accept. I'd lost to classmate, John R. You would have thought that I had just lost a U.S. Presidential election and was facing a life sentence of failure and mediocrity before my peers, but I was a very competitive 17-year old.

Carrying this heavy defeat with me all the way home, I purposefully arrived **after** 5:30 p.m., so I could skip dinner. I was in no mood to share and face my devastating defeat with anyone, my father in particular.

Later that night Ann came up to my room and said Dad wanted to see me downstairs in the living room.

Every muscle in my body clinched.

"About what?" I asked not really wanting the answer.

"You know what," Ann said, "The election."

"What's there to talk about? I got my butt kicked and I lost."

"I know, but you know Dad."

I had no choice. I've already told you about my father, the Marine Corps Colonel with plenty of combat under his belt. How do you tell a man like that, a man whose mantra is IMPROVISE, ADAPT, OVERCOME, that you're *sad* about losing a school election?

As always, the consummate listener, after hearing my 15-minute dissertation on the loss, said simply and calmly (he was always calm under any kind of fire, physical, mental or emotional), "So what are your plans?"

I bowed my head and muttered almost as a question, "Suck it up, I guess and face the music at school tomorrow."

He sat quietly waiting for me to look him in the eye, as he'd always taught us and said, "I understand in two-weeks they are having senior class elections."

It wasn't a question, it was a statement.

I mused to myself, *Hmm, the only way he would have this information was if Ann had told him.*

"Yes, that's right," I said.

"So, do you have plans to **bounce back** and run for Senior Class President?"

"I wasn't planning on it," I said sheepishly.

My father looked me directly in the eyes. He locked on me like a laser guided missile as he always did when he was about to impart a savory piece of wisdom.

"So, after coming within just 18 votes of winning ASB President, you are going to just throw in the towel and now give up?"

Didn't he understand? This wasn't like losing the 880-yard run at a track meet, this was serious! Didn't he understand that second place wasn't an option? Didn't he know I would be humiliated, degraded, looked upon with great disdain? To lose once, ok it wasn't the end of the world, but to lose twice? Are you kidding me? I was scared to death to run again and risk another loss! How could I face my classmates if I lost again? I'd rather transfer to a rival high school for fear of being labeled a two-time loser!

I knew I had to give him an answer though, and quickly.

"I thought about it, but I decided I'm going to kick back and just enjoy my senior year before I head off to college," I said, trying subtly to remind him that I was going to be leaving for college in California in the summer, and needed to "prepare" for the move out west.

My Dad knew that was bull, a weak excuse.

He rubbed his chin as if in deep thought, though I knew from experience he'd already formulated his next response before I'd even finished my excuse.

"I understand," he said calmly. "So, you're going to shut it down, roll up your tent, quit and just coast your senior year?"

He paused for effect.

"That would be disappointing, but if that's your choice, you'll have to live with it."

I knew it was coming. He blew me right out of the water and I knew that wasn't going to be the last I heard from him on that subject, not by a long shot.

For the next two weeks, neither of us spoke a word about the upcoming senior class election. I was walking around the house on eggshells waiting for the second shoe to drop until two weeks later at the dinner table, he blindsided me.

Clanging his water glass with his knife he announced, "I would like to congratulate Shawn on being elected Senior Class President today."

How did he know? Ann had sworn she would not mention a word of it until after I told everyone. Dad said that when he called the school that afternoon to check on the next up-coming track meet, the school secretary had told him the good news.

"Your father knew you were running and he needed to be prepared to support you if you were to come up short," my mom confided in me.

That lesson of getting back up after a defeat, not giving up and going for the second chance opportunity, was a true life lesson experience for me that would serve me well and stay with me the rest of my life. I learned, after a good talk with my father that it would haunt me the rest of my life if I didn't make the effort and I would never have known if I could cut it, if I hadn't run again.

There is no substitute for encouragement when facing a personal challenge, **your fear. There is no substitute for TRUSTED, MEANINGFUL RELATIONSHIPS and powerful teams.**

I could **NOT have done it alone** and would not, if I hadn't had the strong support from my father and sister in my quest for election. My team was with me all the way.

The next day I asked Dad what he would have said had I lost that race. He smiled knowingly; "I would have said that we should hold you back a year and try it all over again," then he threw his arm around me.

After we both shared a big laugh he continued, "Honestly, I don't know what I would have said, but fortunately I didn't have to. We would have crossed that bridge together if we needed to."

I learned a great lesson that year that has always stayed with me. It is a simple. It's a simple lesson that applies to all ages:

There is no substitute for inspiration and encouragement...

when you need to challenge and face your fears. It builds courage, confidence and character and prepares you for the **next opportunities** and challenges that await you. I came up with this one below myself, but it is something my father would certainly agree with.

FEARS AND MISTAKES ARE

LIFE'S BUILDING BLOCKS...

THEY ARE NOT ROAD BLOCKS...embrace them!

SECOND CHANCES...

...that's what mistakes are—opportunities—chances to learn, to grow, to be faster, smarter, more caring, more giving.

Ask yourself, "Where would I be today, if it were not for all the second chance opportunities I was given?" Allow your team members to help you face your fears, follow your dreams and never give up! Then, be there for **them** when they face the same challenges.

The incomparable NBA superstar, **Michael Jordan said,**

Never say never, because limits, like fears, are often just an illusion.

*I **missed** more than **9,000 shots** in my career! I lost almost 300 games. 26 times, **I was trusted** to take the game winning shot and **missed.** I've **failed** over and over and over again in my life. That **is why I succeed.**

Our goals as active trusted team members are to be **difference makers.** You will fail in that role from time to time, just as everyone has, even Michael Jordan, but so will others on your team. Likewise, every member will be successful. When one of you is struggling, some other team member will be picking up the slack whether that's on a work assignment, in the home environment, on the playing field.

Special Teams

Your teams can be vital to our national interest and as complex as a military special warfare team or, it might be as simple as the **South Coast Plaza Walking Team.** This is a team comprised of four very close friends, women who walk together for an hour, five days a week. Their purpose and goal is clear: to experience good low-impact cardio exercise, burn some calories, improve their fitness and share some quality time together.

They began their walking program with 15-minute walks and eventually built up to a solid hour. Their walks started with a single step, one heart beat at a time.

They meet like the clockwork of Big Ben at their designated starting point. They take their walks very seriously and everyone is held accountable for being present.

It's fun, it strengthens their bones and it's a great social interaction—in short, it's a team. They cherish their **3,600 seconds** of quality uninterrupted time (no cell phones or headsets are allowed). They talk about personal issues. They talk about their spouses, children, grandchildren and their communities.

The team consensus is that the **3,600 seconds together** has helped each team member grow in the areas of health, self-awareness, communication, companionship and resolving challenges.

This special one hour a day team commitment continues to transform and grow each of them every day of their lives.

P.S. *Each of the team members is 80+years old!*

P.P.S. *It is not revealed how far they walk, but the distance isn't important. Perhaps it's only two miles for all we know, but they do it together and they do it for one hour. IN ADDITION, they do it five days a week, every week of the year.*

What will you do with 3,600 seconds tomorrow?

We Can't Do It Alone
Another Special Team Story

*We **WANT** to be in a situation under maximum pressure, maximum intensity, and maximum danger. When it's shared with others, it provides a bond, which is stronger than any tie that can exist.*
--Navy SEAL Team Six Member

In this book, there is a clear reason why the word **TEAM** appears more than any other. We all know or will soon learn that WE CAN'T DO IT ALONE.

(According to a recent article in the *Journal of Sports Sciences*, "The researchers found that players who thought about their team's strengths felt more confident and performed better than those who focused on personal strengths.

Emphasizing the group may ease your performance anxiety so you can relax and focus.")

More importantly, those committed team members who are currently living a passionate and positive H2G daily disciplined plan to build trusted relationships, are already experiencing the growth, happiness and success benefits of this special relationship journey. **(You will discover the H2G Revolution in the next chapter.)**

The H2G universal mission statement is:

To inspire humanity one person, one relationship, and one Team at a time by adopting and LIVING a passionate and positive H2G, Head, Heart and Gut mental, emotional, physical, and spiritual mindset with a daily disciplined plan to build trusted relationships to achieve individual and team growth, happiness and success.

CEO Howard Schultz inspired me with Starbuck's corporate mission statement: "To inspire and nurture the human spirit, one person, one cup and one neighborhood at a time." Thank you Howard and thank your team for their pro-active work in their communities as **Change Agents.**

Most of us really want to be part of a team. Just think of all the important teams you are either a part of, or would like to have in your life. They are all unique and all serve a special purpose in our lives.

Our role as pro-active CHANGE AGENTS is to be an active member and a difference maker in changing and improving lives and building meaningful and trusted relationships.

The big question: What is or will be your commitment level to your team? Are you just looking to cruise along and put in your time just to say you're on the **team**? Or, are you looking to totally connect and commit to a **team** that you will feed and will feed you? Are you being fully responsible and accountable as a contributing team member? Are you a *passionate* and *positive warrior* purposefully driven to serve your team every day, reap the personal, and team benefits of growth, happiness and success?

Whatever team you are on, become a part of, or desire to create, that team needs to be all about individual team members' growth, happiness and success at the end of the day. If everyone is genuinely caring, sharing and giving, the journey will be meaningful and beneficial to all.

The U.S. Navy Seal Teams and any hospital ER Team are two of what I call **EXTREME** teams. Since they are extremes, much of what they are faced with and accomplish can only be held up as a model, but their teamwork is instructive because they are already living within the most trusted relationships we can imagine.

Both teams have all the active ingredients of H_2G as will be revealed shortly. They deal every day with time sensitive and life-threatening challenges at work.

These trained professional teams know too well that if they did not have a team built on trusted relationships, their mission would fail and lives could be lost. Without a trusted relationship, their success as a team would not be consistent. It would only be random, and lucky. This is clearly not good enough and unacceptable for **these** two extreme teams.

The U.S. Navy Seal Teams, considered one of most
advanced special warfare military teams in the world, has a brotherhood connection and relationship that is rare and ironclad. It was designed that way.

Their team relationship is the definition of **UNCONDITIONAL TRUST**. Each individual, after **earning** the elite passage and honor to become a member is unselfishly committed to serve and protect every other member.

Every SEAL is totally prepared during EVERY mission to sacrifice his own life for his fellow team member and mission and though chances are you'll never be faced with that kind of sacrifice, it is the epitome of a meaningful and trusted relationship.

I have known many of these honorable public servants and have spoken with them at length about their loyalty, trust and relationships to each other. Their highly advanced mental, physical and emotional team training is a unique, one-of-a kind connection. It is a membership that is desired only by a handful who are committed to serving our country.

Like the SEALS, emergency room operating teams, are constantly facing high-risk time sensitive, life and death assignments. Their skill-set requires critical understanding, assessment, and competent and courageous execution every day.

Every day they "prepare for battle," **manage and overcome fear** with their mastery of the Gut. During the decisive moment, under fire and often with uncertainty and chaos staring them in the face, they have prepared to succeed AND believe and know they will! They believe failure is not an option and they will battle to the very end.

Often times we hear or read about these highly competent, courageous teams humbly saying, "It went our way today," or "We were lucky today, it all worked out well for us." While this may be the case from time to time, it's really all about THEM making it happen with a passionate and positive

H$_2$G attitude believing and trusting in each other and unselfishly committing to carrying out the team's mission one minute, one hour, and one day at a time.

Like all teams, a successful outcome is never guaranteed but the opportunity for growth is always there as long as we know and understand we have a commitment to working together and serving each other every day—extreme or otherwise.

You may not face these types of extreme situations, but your goals can still be the same.

Fear, courage and freedom

Just looking at the word fear conjures up a little anxiety. It instantly reminds us of something we were worrying about, some distasteful task we are supposed to perform: meeting a company deadline, your child's safety, your spouse's failing health. There is one thing certain in this world; fear is never in short supply.

Every one of us has personally experienced fear and knows someone close to us who has faced or is living with some type of controlling fear in his or her life; fear of rejection, criticism, loneliness, success, failure—the list is practically endless. Many of these unresolved and buried fears date back to our early childhood years. However, there are also many fears we have managed and conquered that have strengthened our courage and confidence.

Fear can control you emotionally and physically and even be so debilitating, it can destroy your health and life.

The real question is: **HOW do we begin to address, understand, manage and overcome these fears** so we can live more meaningful and happy lives?

None of us can truly do it alone. I hope that you have this memorized by now. The solution is: YOUR TEAMS. We all need to be connected and part of a trusted relationship team that will help us to understand the fears that are holding us back, and then support us in facing the fears head on. Once we understand the fears and get the support to confront them we can get the courage to face those fears head on. **From Fears To Freedom.**

Earlier I said, "Fear is a building block, an opportunity. It shouldn't be viewed as a roadblock or dead end. Fear can be a good thing, and in fact, thousands of years ago…

FEAR WAS NECESSARY FOR SURVIVAL…

50,000 years ago, Paleolithic man was surrounded by fear. In a way, **all he or she had was FEAR and TRUSTED TEAMS.** Everything to these earliest humans was a threat, from saber tooth tigers to disease. Paleolithic man lived in two distinct modes: fight or flight (lots of cortisol coursing through his veins and organs causing untold stress on his body or, the occasional respite probably enjoyed for only very brief hours in the day with a tribal member or members.

Early man did not live alone.

From the moment they realized their own existence, they found safety in numbers. I guess we can assume these were the first trusted, meaningful relationships and it proves that this is the way we are meant to live.

Fear drove these tribes to hunt and live together.

THE POWER OF TEAM.

Of course, as humankind progressed, living in constant fear was NOT NECESSARY to survival—but TEAMS always were. Unfortunately today, in our hectic, techno driven, striving culture, we still manage to have plenty of the old fight or flight left buried in our genes even though there aren't many Saber tooth tigers roaming the parking lots at the grocery store.

In most cases, you are not in a fight for your life even though at some given moment, it may seem like it. Most fears are created in our own minds. They are merely "perceptions." In fact, most of what we call STRESS, is nothing more than our own perception of people, places or events. PERCEIVED STRESSORS can be identified and discarded like the wrapper from a package of gum.

The mind is powerful. We all have a wonderful capacity for creativity. In fact, it is one of the driving forces in our lives. The great American author and change agent Napoleon Hill, best describes the power of the mind when he wrote: **"What the mind can conceive and believe, it can achieve."**

I talk a lot about FEAR in this book because one of the most successful ways to deal with it, as we have already seen, is to recognize it and welcome it into your life. I know it's not easy. When you are feeling fearful, embrace it. Invite it in and say, "I am not afraid of you. You are an illusion. You are the result of my vivid imagination, nothing more.

That is how you **FACE your FEARS.**

And, of course, you have the help of a TRUSTED and MEANINGFUL RELATIONSHIP team member. Look at fear as an **opportunity** to learn more about yourself and the world around you. See it as a building block. Experience it as something new and important you never would have learned if you had remained fearful. Share it with your trusted team. Do not be embarrassed or ashamed that you fear something no matter how small.

Success is never final, failure is never fatal. It's courage that counts.

--John Wooden

In 2012, while attending a personal development workshop in Los Angeles with my friend Joe, I was surprised to hear and learn of all the fears participants openly identified and shared: "I will end up not being 'good enough,' and, "I'm afraid that people will discover that weakness." They also shared, "My parents reminded me that I wasn't good enough growing up. I'm afraid I will not live up to what is expected of me."

More surprising to me was learning how many of those executives and managers grew up in an environment that reinforced the idea that they couldn't do IT or weren't good enough.

WOW. I also learned, but wasn't surprised that many of their shared fears were currently adversely affecting their work performance and business relationships.

Their fears included: work performance, being constantly graded and micro-managed, fear of presenting a group project and fear of being called upon in a management meeting to express their position and/or opinion.

Many also admitted those fears seriously held them back in life and created a mindset of low confidence, inadequacy and inferiority.

Fear of failure, fear of criticism and fear of public speaking were the top three fears identified. All three are emotional "growth stoppers" in any company culture and any individual mind. We must remember: real growth happens with mistakes and failures and what **we learn from them.**

A good friend of mine who overcame a monumental fear told me, "Fear and mistakes are the manure that grows success and happiness. They both stink, but they fertilize the mind."

Growing up, my parents always reminded us that the opportunity was there for us to do and be anything we wanted in this world, as long as we put in the necessary hard work, committed to never giving up, and had the real courage to always tackle and overcome any obstacles, big or small.

They both taught me that most fear and failure was just a temporary state of mind as long as we confronted and tackled it head on, as long as we KNEW it was only a temporary PERCEPTION. If we ignored it, denied it, or ran from it, the fear would only grow along with resentment and insecurities.

Understanding public speaking is widely recognized as one of the biggest fears most people have. I want to share another personal childhood story where my parents introduced us to this very fear, which turned out to be a great **growth opportunity** for the entire family.

Public speaking 101

The human brain starts working the moment you are born and never stops, until you stand up to speak in public.

--George Jessel

As I have related, in the Cassidy home, all nine of us had dinner together promptly at 5:30 p.m., or we didn't eat. From 5:30 to 6:00 p.m., we went around the table taking turns sharing our daily school experiences. From 6:00 to 6:30 p.m., all seven kids, Mom and Dad engaged in an open discussion and debate on current affairs and politics.

We were all expected to be up on the news of the day and prepared to articulate and debate a position. This routine, with plenty of heated dinner debates, was so instrumental for us all in building communication skills and confidence. It was something we all actually looked forward to and prepared for. Our dinner conversations were like a continuous presidential debate that never ended. The only difference was that we didn't have to dress up and have scripted partisan talking points.

To build our skills and confidence in communication and public speaking, Mom and Dad required all the kids to enter and compete in the junior high school oration contest. This was an eight to 10 minute memorized "original oratory" (open topic) speech. It was a very big annual event at school and **THE** speaking event in the Cassidy household.

Dad would always say that public speaking is feared by most because it's an acquired skill that takes a ton of practice and very few of us ever do enough of it to be good. He also believed the best way to conquer this fear was to compete in public speaking and practice for hours on end.

Mom was a masterful speechwriter and Dad was a passionate speech coach. Mom would spend countless hours teaching us how to research, structure and write a solid speech.

In preparation for the competition, it was very common for us to present and practice our speech in front of the family (troops) for two to three hours a night—two consecutive weeks in a row!

When one of us was preparing for the big competition, the rest of us all sat on the living room couch as judges. We would take notes, dissecting every word, voice fluctuation, tone variation and body gesture. After the speech was delivered, three or four times, we would all openly offer up our constructive comments. Mom and Dad would summarize the group critique and decide what comments were worthy to keep and incorporate. It wasn't uncommon for our speeches to be presented five or six times in any given night.

Dad, who was a huge admirer of the great football coach Vincent Lombardi, would always remind us of what he called the greatest "competitor preparedness" quote of all time: "Practice does not make perfect. Only perfect practice makes perfect."

While we thought that he demanded perfection in our performance, he always reminded us that being perfect was rarely ever achieved; we just needed to be closer to perfection than our opponent was if we expected to win.

There is a reason symphony orchestras, Olympic professionals, college sports, special military and medical surgical teams to name a few, practice, train and prepare so hard striving to make their performances perfect. Championships are won by teams that have excellent preparedness and have **perfected practice**.

This life lesson and speaking competition served us well. It all started with Brenda, the oldest, setting the bar by winning 1st place in her very first high school speech competition when we were living in Oceanside, California.

From 1971 through 1974, the four years we lived in Lee Summit, Missouri, Ann, Colleen, Kathy and I all won first place in the school oration competition.

That early introduction to public speaking was a great childhood and life confidence booster for all the kids.

Fortunately we had two parents who were passionately committed to see their kids not only learn and develop the fundamentals of public speaking and debating, but to inspire us to prepare, practice and **ALWAYS** learn as a **TEAM**: Unus pro omnibus, omnes pro uno. All for one, one for all. Each one of us, as a committed team member, was obsessed with the other member's success.

This was an ongoing lesson of how we can USE fear to our advantage. The endless practices were the **FACING** of it. It's not until we can understand, manage and in many cases, overcome our fears, that we can truly realize and celebrate life's biggest treasure of happiness:

FREEDOM.

The best adaptive company cultures and top college sports programs totally understand how much growth comes from mistakes and failures. They also understand company and team leaders must give their employees and players a green light to take risk and fail. By giving permission to remove the fear of failure, organizations and team members will only grow and thrive.

The thing you fear most has no power. Your fear of it is what has the power. Facing the truth really will set you free.
-- Oprah Winfrey

Growing up I was fortunate to experience a number of personal fear and failure lessons. These experiences, at the time, all seemed bigger than life for me. I had NO idea how life changing those fears and courage lessons would later play in my personal and business life.

All the seeds were being planted for my adult H_2G plan.

It's time for the H_2G Revolution!

**Thoughts to remember for
Chapter Three: The Power of Teams**

- A team is **two or more people.**

- YOU ARE NEVER ALONE

-NBA star basketball player, Michael Jordan summed it up best when he wrote about a common belief we share, **"My heroes are and were my parents. I can't see having anyone else as my heroes."**

-IMPROVISE, ADAPT, and OVERCOME...a good philosophy for anyone.

-There is no substitute for inspiration and encouragement...

-FEARS AND MISTAKES ARE

LIFE'S BUILDING BLOCKS...

THEY ARE NOT ROAD BLOCKS...embrace them!

-Practice does not make perfect. Only perfect practice makes perfect.

-We must remember: real growth happens with mistakes and failures and what we learn from them.

-A friend of mine who overcame a monumental fear told me, "Fear and mistakes are the manure that grows success and happiness. They both stink, but they fertilize the mind."

-One for all and all for one.

NOTES:

I encourage you to write your thoughts in this space. Make note of some action items you want to remember. This will fire up your Head, Heart and Gut as you begin the H$_2$G Revolution.

Chapter Four
The H₂G Revolution

Man is but the product of his thoughts. What he thinks, he becomes. Be the change you want to see in the world.

--Mahatma Gandhi

We've talked so far about the importance **and power of trusted relationships** and I think we can all agree that they are the most important things in our lives.

I've spoken about the **7 Step Relationship Ladder**, and all the attributes of people who are seeking to develop and nurture truly meaningful relationships:

**likeability,
understanding,
competency,
opportunity,
respect, trust, and unconditional trust.**

Before we return to the subject of meaningful relationships however, **it is time to discover how you can find,**
develop
and nurture
these kinds of relationships.

It's fine to talk about what trusted relationships are and why they are so important but it is altogether different to talk about how to implement them.

What can you do on a daily basis, as not only a plan, but also a new mind-set and lifestyle that will allow you to build, improve and grow these important relationships in your life and the lives of others?

I have the secret. It is called H$_2$G. I truly believe that if you begin to **live** this plan on a daily basis (not just give it lip service), not only will you be happier, fulfilled and more successful in your personal and business life, but by **living** this plan, you will **become** what I call a passionate "change agent," much like what Gandhi spoke of:

Man is but the product of his thoughts. What he thinks, he becomes. Be the change you want to see in the world.

By living the **H$_2$G plan** 365 days a year, growing your own understanding of what trusted relationships are and why they are so important as well as growing yourself as a person, disciplining yourself, you will become a beacon to all the **teams** in your world: family, spiritual, business, community, charity—all of them small or large.

Living the **H$_2$G plan** will transform you and everyone who meets you. Influential business people, religious figures, diplomats, teachers and mentors talk about the influences we can exert in our own lives by *being* **the change we want to see.**

We are all woven together regardless of the color of our

skin, our religion, politics or business. Whether we are male or female, old or young makes no difference. We cannot expect others to work with us as teammates, or to invest their time, energies and emotions in us, if we do not start in our own homes—this physical, mental, emotional, spiritual body in which we all exist.

Our success in happiness and fulfillment is inexplicably woven into the success of others in our relationships.

The **H₂G plan** and lifestyle is based on you and starts with *you.* You are the vessel that will become compassionate, understanding, and trusted that you will become a powerful agent for change in the world starting one person at a time in your own family, job, community and beyond.

All journeys (physical, mental, emotional, spiritual) begin with the first thought and the first step!

You have the opportunity to become that agent of change through your self-generated enthusiasm, your energy, your purpose, your focus, your positive attitude and outlook on everything in your world. **Trust me, you will find almost immediately, that people will be drawn to you and your ideas like a moth to the light.** You will become contagious (in a positive way of course).

H₂G is the acronym for this vessel of yours:

From your Head to your Heart and your Gut

The core of this H₂G plan is:

*Adopting and **living** a passionate and positive: **Head, Heart** and **Gut** mind-set and lifestyle.*

This is your mental, emotional and physical mindset, using a 365-day a year-disciplined **plan to build trusted relationships** to achieve individual and team growth, happiness and success.

Your HEAD, HEART and GUT are your keys to the kingdom. In other words, you already have it in you to be a world-class **change agent**, a constructive and positive difference maker.

Can you imagine what would be possible if we all seriously committed to working on developing and exercising some critical and powerful components within our brain and heart that may have been lying dormant for years? We could literally be guaranteed a more fulfilled and meaningful life through our relationships.

I want to share with you how adopting and living this formula will build, expand and strengthen your mind, heart, confidence and character as a human being, which in turn is going to forever change every relationship in your life and beyond.

It is commonly understood that we are strongly influenced by those people we respect, admire and trust AND those who genuinely **care** about us. We all desire to be accepted, recognized and complimented on a job well done. In the words of Mary Kay Ash, founder of Mary Kay Cosmetics,

There are only two things in this world more powerful than sex and money: praise and recognition.

William James reinforces this human desire and emotion, with his powerful quote:

The deepest principle of human nature is the craving to be appreciated.

We all desire to be the best we can be. If we are going to be the finest at whatever we choose to become, we need that passionate and committed team member and mentor to help us. We cannot do it alone.

Every world leader in every conceivable discipline whether that is the corporate world, politics, military, religion or education, had mentors who inspired, taught, and supported them through the critical and necessary H$_2$G components that I will be outlining, even though they did not refer to it that way.

You cannot do it alone.

Remember, a team is just two or more. Neither you, nor any successful people you know or have read about have ever done it alone—no one! You and your spiritual leader (on call 24-7) qualify as a great two-member team!

Unfortunately, in our current culture, many people are raised and taught that it's all about them, the individual. Many of us have been programmed early on to listen to that one radio station in life: **"WIIFM." What's in it for me?** Some people will never change living this lonely and selfish lifestyle.

We all know too many people who experienced or are experiencing this broken, sad, and lonely lifestyle, one that involves little or no real meaningful relationships. It makes it particularly tough when it's an immediate family member.

There are others who will wake up one day, perhaps after reading this book and understanding **H$_2$G** and will have the biggest "aha" moment of their lives and they will begin to understand that the fulfilled life is truly about caring, sharing and serving. They will learn it's not all about them. Love must be given away. You cannot save it for a rainy day.

Those that have that 150-watt light bulb go on over their heads will finally realize that we are all part of each other. Our success, our rights, our desires are so tightly connected to one another; we cannot continue to swim upstream through the river of humanity.

Allow me to introduce and explain the critical living components of H₂G and show you examples of how it works and how it can positively affect and change your life. Then, I will present you with a daily plan to implement and internalize all you are about to read.

H₂G
Head, Heart, Gut

HEAD

Everything starts with the mind or Head "H," the mysterious, complex and magical mind. It is fascinating that the average human brain weighs just three pounds, which is mostly water (78%) and has 80 to **100 billion cells** (neurons) , which is close to the same number of stars in our Galaxy.

Our average three-pound "miracle worker" processes 50-60,000 thoughts a day. According to top neuroscientists, two-thirds of all those thoughts are somehow related to fear in one way or another!

Our brain makes up and processes all our thinking, reasoning, intelligence, ideas, feelings, perceptions, attitudes, memory, will and judgments.

It's hard to believe this small watery organ represents our **complete, complex conscious and unconscious mind** and that it directs, influences and controls our mental, emotional, physical, and spiritual behavior—completely.

The major ingredients or living components that make up the "H" or Head in H$_2$G are:

self, purpose, positive attitude, focus, effective communicator, critical and strategic thinker, core competency, team player, relationship builder, and full-time student.

It all begins with self. It begins with you knowing what your strengths and weaknesses are. "He who knows others is wise. He who knows *himself* is enlightened."- Loa-Tzu

Once we have a true and deep understanding of ourselves, we can seek and engage in a **purpose**-filled life. We all need to have purpose if we expect to live a meaningful and fulfilling life full of purpose and passion.

In order to grow, you need to discover your real purpose in life. It is imperative that you find that collected mind and heart emotion that tells you this is what I am here for, this is my calling. Pursue the purpose that captures your heart. This is the beginning of real change and growth. Once you know yourself, you will begin to become a change agent. You will be that difference maker.

One of my personal favorite modern day change agent role models is Jane Goodall. This world-renowned primatologist and humanitarian, has spent her entire life working with chimpanzees and creating global awareness for the environment. She is the definition and role model of someone living a purpose-driven life and conveys it so well when she describes her mission in life: "Every day has to count. Every day I want to learn something. Every day I want to be inspired. Every day I want to inspire someone."

To me, that says it all!

However, please do not get the impression that you have to do something as dramatic as moving to Africa to become a change agent. You can become a potent force for change right in your own home, at work, on any team you belong to. It all begins with one step. Like the uninformed man asked the wise man, "How do you eat an elephant?" The wise man replied, "One bite at a time." It's as simple as talking to your neighbor—one person, one simple step.

I have a good friend who is 65 years old and is still adamant that he accomplish two vital things every day...no matter what. To him, every day that he does not learn something and accomplish something is a sad lost opportunity. He is like a sponge for knowledge and understanding and he is driven to be productive in his chosen field as a writer—every single day. His first passion is writing but intertwined with that purpose is his thirst for knowledge and productivity and though he works alone, he has become a part of many teams that he enjoys, depends upon and contributes to. He won't cure cancer, nor win the Nobel Prize for peace, but he is making a difference in his world. He has joined the H_2G revolution! He is a certified Change Agent.

A positive attitude

The next vital living ingredient in Head is **Positive Attitude.** We have all heard the saying that attitude is everything and that is so true.

The positive mental attitude component is critical and essential. A positive attitude can lead and fast track you to happiness and success and can change your entire life. A sour outlook will repel everyone you meet. Remember the Trust Ladder. The first step is likeability. It is hard to like someone who is always negative, whining or complaining. If you are hard to like, it will be difficult to be part of a team.

It's not easy to maintain that positive attitude in high gear, but if you are going to be a genuine change agent and make a real difference to influence others in a highly charged, positive way, you must embrace it, display it **and live it daily.**

Your own change takes a constant and consistent **positive mental attitude** every day. With all the negatives we are bombarded with in the media daily, we must constantly work to focus on creating and living a positive mental mind set EVERY DAY.

If you look and focus on the bright side of life, and all you are grateful for, your whole being becomes filled with energy, happiness, growth, and far more inner strength. A positive attitude motivates and inspires us and the way we look at the world. It also affects our entire environment and all the people around us. If it is strong and persistent enough, it becomes **contagious**.

How do we keep a positive attitude? We must exercise it every day!

Now, after identifying the **H₂G HEAD** components of **self, purpose, positive attitude, focus, effective communicator, critical and strategic thinker, core competency, team player, relationship builder, and full-time student,** just think about how powerful and important real **effective communication** is in the HEAD and in every facet of your life.

The more we can become aware of the critical need to communicate effectively and become truly engaged as emotional listeners, the more we are making an enormous amount of progress and growth.

The critical importance and power of effective communication cannot be understated! It can be informative, persuasive, inspiring, and motivating. When communication is broken, misunderstood, manipulated, or one-sided, we all know the likely outcome—we experience, mistrust, fear, insecurity, failed systems and failed outcomes.

Communication is the two-way street of conveying and receiving. The communicator needs to convey his/her message to the listener and the listener needs to receive the message. Is it that simple? No, it is a very complicated process and is one of our biggest life challenges in both our personal and business lives.

Only in a perfect world, would there be little or no misunderstanding, misinterpretation, or miscommunication. More often than not, we are not communicating to others effectively. Many of the things we say or try to convey are incomplete, unclear and often are ignored.

My mom, the late Elizabeth "Betty" Cassidy, always taught us growing up her 95-5 rule: "Ninety-five percent of the world 'communicates,' the **other** five percent communicate effectively."

Effective communication is actually an artful skill-set we can all work at to improve daily.

Critical and strategic thinking

We all need to be H_2G **critical and strategic thinkers**. We cannot just absorb and accept everything coming our way and continue to simply react to all the challenges that impact our daily lives. Rather, we need to take action. We need to **think**, understand, and address the events, moments and situations in our environment if we hope to have a chance of being productive and successful in dealing with our daily priorities and challenges.

Once we seriously engage in the strategic and critical thought process, we are immediately reminded that we cannot do it alone.

Core competency

The next powerful ingredient in the HEAD is **core competency.** Knowledge, integrity, expertise, experience, commitment, and results are all key elements that lead to long-term growth and success. It is worth repeating that your commitment and demonstration to being the best of the best on your team and in your relationships is everything! It is one of the most powerful, influential, meaningful and necessary elements in building trust and opening doors for opportunity in your relationships.

Team Player

In order to live the H₂G plan, we need to be **Team Players** committed to building and supporting our valued relationships! In order to do this, we must commit to being **full-time students** and teachers of growth. Again, we must be constantly and consistently open to learning and growing-whether at your home kitchen table, classroom, workplace, playing field, on your computer, or on the street; we all need to be full- time students.

Author Alvin Toffler gives us a powerful wake-up call when he writes: *The illiterate of the 21ˢᵗ century will not be those who cannot read, but those who cannot learn, unlearn and re-learn.*

We all need to constantly question, expand and develop our minds—if we are not growing; we are losing ground and regressing.

Clearly the new technology revolution, now expanding even to rural towns and villages, is the biggest game changer for every person or group in the world—the ability to "communicate" instantaneously to nearly every person on earth! This is a phenomenon some would call a "Tipping Point," in the ability to converse in real time, all the time with billions of people. Imagine how easy it is today to become a change agent when you can spread the word instantly via the internet.

A **team player** who is contributing is a person who craves more knowledge, and is anxious to build his team with this knowledge at every opportunity.

In this new, complex and ever changing world, we must remind ourselves that learning every day is an absolute must and is a critical component of the Head in H_2G.

Remember all the components in the Head start with **self**. That is the only place that: **purpose, positive attitude, focus, effective communicator, critical and strategic thinker, competent and competitive team member, team builder, and full-time student** resides.

H_2G
Head, Heart, Gut

Heart

The second component of H_2G is your **Heart**. After understanding the components of the **Head,** we need to connect the other part of the vessel that is you: the **Heart.** The human heart has four chambers. The average heart weighs only 7 to 15 ounces, and is about the size of an average human fist.

The **Heart** in H_2G is an ANALOGY for the **four critical components** that reside in the four chambers of the HEART.

The four chambers of our H₂G Heart are:

1　**The Passionate Warrior**
2　**Empathy and Faith**
3　**Generosity and Gratitude**
4　**Reflection and Forgiveness**

Within the first chamber of the HEART is the **Passionate Warrior.**

In order to be a true change agent, you must be that **Passionate Warrior** and be mentally, physically, emotionally and spiritually on fire with desire to be an impact team member. The Passionate Warrior is always prepared, dedicated, loyal, and courageous in setting the performance bar, in serving the cause and in building trusted team relationships.

Your **passion** is the power that **drives you**. It stimulates your conscious mind. What exactly does that mean? The essence of the H₂G daily regimen (more on that later with the H₂G/365 day plan), is to become a beacon in all your team relationships. It is **setting the example** through your behavior and deeds: **showing** people, not **telling** them.

If you live your daily life through the tenets of H₂G, you become stronger in mind, heart and body, which in turn become extremely obvious to everyone around you and begins to rub off on them. You become contagious but with great humility. Remember, H₂G is not about preaching, it's about doing, sharing, inspiring, empowering, serving and living those changes you want to see. You are always a team member first. In this manner, and only in this sincere and genuine manner, will you actually be working to build and create trusted meaningful relationships. In essence, you are simultaneously the mentor and the protégé—teaching and learning as you develop.

We all know that no one wants to be in the company of a phony self-serving individual. Most people love to be part of a team of passionate warriors. Teams of passionate warriors lead social, political, economic, religious and technological changes, movements and revolutions throughout the world that are life changing! They influence politicians, fight for the cause, build institutions, create new markets, save children, leave legacies, value and protect traditions, win championships.

Next, be courageous in your decisions. Passionate warriors are truthful and forthright all the time. Say what you mean and mean what you say. Do not dance around uncomfortable situations. Being direct and sincere works best. Be the go to person, the one people know they can count on for action, truth and results.

Empathy and Faith

The second chamber in the H_2G **HEART** is **EMPATHY** and **FAITH**.

These become part of your every fiber. People know when you are genuine or not. If you are, it's because you are a caring and understanding individual. The easiest way to exercise and strengthen this heart "muscle" is simply by using the Golden Rule in every interaction. By asking yourself how you want to be treated and then dealing with others in your home and workplace, continually and consistently day in and day out in this manner, you ARE sincere. You are caring. You are compassionate. You are understanding and everyone will always trust that. The ability to empathize, to truly understand and share the real feelings, thoughts and situations of another, is a special and needed ingredient in the HEART.

Can you begin to see how these types of H_2G "exercises" work in drawing those around you in work or play to a complimentary mindset? You become contagious because you are REAL and people feel your passion, strength and optimism and they begin to mirror your examples.

The next chamber in the Heart is **FAITH.** Faith is so much more than believing and counting on the job getting done, successfully closing the deal, meeting or exceeding your company's quarterly growth forecast. It's a faith in a Higher Power! I believe that we all need to embrace that higher power, that entity that we can call on and count on. No matter what religion or spiritual moral compass you follow, your faith in a chosen belief is needed and necessary to keep us real, to keep us grounded, humble and focused on serving.

Believers in a higher power know that without their faith, they would be lost, empty and hopeless, giving up on living a meaningful and fulfilled life. They also clearly know and accept that they are not perfect and they know **they can never do it alone.**

For those who believe, practice and live their faith every day, there is **no stronger** and more meaningful relationship than their spiritual high power. The miraculous power of a strong faith has no equal and is available to each of us on call 24 hours a day! It is an extremely contagious and powerful HEART ingredient in building trusted and meaningful relationships with your team members.

Generosity and Gratitude

The third chamber of the HEART is **GENEROSITY** and **GRATITUDE.** We often think of generosity and gratitude when we see people coming together to help innocent victims and their loved ones during times of great need. There are also many individuals and great charity teams generously giving and serving worldwide to support poverty, cures for disease, wounded veterans, crime victims, children's needs. Nothing strengthens the Heart muscle like unconditional giving.

Each one of us should take 15 minutes out of our day to express our gratitude to someone who has positively impacted our lives, or teams. Can you imagine the real difference and growth we can achieve in our relationships? The greatest gift is love and the greatest feeling and emotional reward is when we are openly and unconditionally giving. The good news is your actions, attitudes and feelings become **contagious!**

I would like to share a powerful gratitude experience in my life last year that propelled me to ACT and recognize a special individual with his employer. It is an everyday business with everyday employees doing simple jobs like preparing and serving food.

This story can be best summarized in my letter below to the CEO of the fast food chicken chain below. I have changed the employee's name and store location for privacy purposes.

Mr. Steve S.
President and CEO
El Pollo Loco

Dear Mr. S.:

I have been a loyal customer of El Pollo Loco for over 13 years and frequent your ----------, CA store 2 days a week as a regular. An interesting note: I was actually first introduced to El Pollo Loco in 1981 at your first U.S. store location in Los Angeles while I was a student at USC.

I wanted to bring an important matter to your attention. It's not a food quality or pricing issue or an employee complaint, it's an issue I know every company CEO would proudly welcome on a daily basis if it came across his or her desk.

While your overall food quality and customer service at your store is consistently excellent, ONE "Difference Maker" employee is over the top and nothing short of an El Pollo Loco customer service role model for your Company. Jose, who I had the distinct pleasure to meet at the store over 7 years ago, truly understands and demonstrates the essence of customer service.

As President of a leading conference/lodging resort destination and as a financial and marketing consultant with

27 years' experience, I certainly understand and appreciate the critical role and difference quality customer service serves in retaining customers and building customer loyalty.

In my 8-year experience with Jose, I have ONLY witnessed one look and one attitude from him: a beaming smile of generosity, of gratitude and a "Service First" Attitude! From greeting me with an open door to re-wiping my table to filling my ice tea drink WITH lemon, to serving up my favorite salsa from the salsa bar, he is consistently there 100% of the time to offer and provide an unmatched level of customer service. Any 5-Star fine steak or seafood restaurant would be fortunate to have ONE "Jose" on their team who demonstrates his "customer care" passion and commitment.

I have taken many clients and friends to this location for lunch and dinner. After our experience with Jose, they would often ask me if I was related to Jose or if I owned the store franchise. After quickly learning neither was the case, they would all be taken back with Jose's outstanding customer care and his genuine over-the-top friendly attitude.

What sparked me to write this long overdue and deserving letter of recognition? I have been very blessed and fortunate to receive many thank you letters from satisfied clients in my industry over the years. I recently received a letter that not only reminded me just how important customer service is, but the personal REWARD and fulfillment I received when the customer took the time to express his sincere appreciation in writing to me—made my day! I humbly include my letter to you, only to demonstrate the impact of this customer's heartfelt appreciation of customer service and to let you KNOW that I, along with my team, will always use Jose's customer care service and attitude as a model to emulate every day!

I will always be grateful for the "Jose Experience" at El Pollo Loco and can only look forward to meeting other customer care experts in the service sector who have Jose's passion.

Regards,

Shawn Cassidy

I learned that the CEO and members of his executive team drove down from their corporate offices to the San Diego area store to formally recognize Jose before his peers the day he received my letter.

Jose was awarded a special customer service gold pin in the presence of all his peers, including his grandson, who works at the store. I heard it was a very emotional experience for everyone, mostly for Jose. When I learned Jose was not able to read my letter in English, I had a dear friend of mine, retype my letter in Spanish so I could personally present it to him.

I sincerely commend CEO Steve S. for taking the time to make that special trip down to recognize and praise Jose for his dedicated customer service. I know it meant everything to Jose and changed his life.

I have developed a H2G customer "Service First" model that I have lived by for over 25 years. While I have devoted a chapter to share on this topic later in the book, it is important to understand that being the Passionate Warrior like Jose is: **Everything!**

When CEO's **make** the time to personally recognize and praise their front line employees for outstanding performance, nothing serves to build companywide TEAM morale faster and stronger from top to bottom in any organization.

Jose's grandson told me later that his grandfather was grateful for my "generosity" and that he had never been recognized or received any award in his entire life. I told his grandson that I am the lucky one, the proud and grateful recipient of his grandfather's generous service and special friendship for 8 years. As long as Jose is working at El Pollo Loco, I will always be a loyal customer.

Every day let us remember and celebrate all that we are grateful for and all those who have generously taught us, mentored us, befriended us, coached us, served us, prayed with and for us, played with, danced with us, protected and loved us.

Reflection and Forgiveness

The fourth chamber of the HEART is **Reflection** and **Forgiveness.**

Reflection begins every day with what I call, "setting your mind" and "feeling your heart" before your day gets started.

Set aside just 30 minutes every morning before you start your "official" day. Find a quiet place without any phones, computers or televisions—no distractions, no interruptions, only you. This is **your "Reflection"** time.

This is where the strongest sense of **self** begins by quietly reflecting. This is your quality time for prayer, meditation and serious introspection. This is a time where we all need to be in a calm, cool and collected state of total stability or equanimity—getting into your own **head first** before you interact with others.

During this time, the brain is not reacting, fighting or working in overdrive. It's a time for deep thought, relaxation and a time to slow everything down before your typical rat race day begins, a time to be fully in the present.

This is a special time for you to feed your brain, heart and soul. These 30 minutes may also be the only quiet time you'll have with yourself all day.

You will soon discover that it is well worth getting up that extra half-hour early even if you're not a morning person. Look at it as a treat, not an exercise. View it as a fresh new beginning. This is your time. You did not steal it from anyone or anything. You saved it for you.

This is how you can use some of that extra

FOUR HOURS (14,400 seconds)
each day that you were wasting
worrying,
trying to get the better of someone else in an argument,
regretting something that is long past,
etc., etc., etc.

For those who regularly experience this special time of meditation, prayer and introspection, no explanation is needed to describe just how beneficial and refreshing this is. It grounds you, it centers you, if fulfills you. This time makes all the difference in how you face your day.

For those who will be taking on this new experience, I promise you, you'll get so caught up into treating yourself with this unique time you'll likely end up pushing that 30 minutes to an hour.

I also promise you that this time will begin to work miracles elsewhere in your life, eventually it will help feed your soul, and it will help you heal, gain perspective, build confidence and most importantly, bring **clarity!** There is nothing quite as exhilarating, mind-expanding or peace inducing as clarity. It is where dreams come into sharp focus and where they magically turn into action and reality.

I saw this miracle in my own son, Jordan, at the end of our one-year program of exile. For the first time in his crazy roller coaster ride of more than seven years, he had pure clarity. He knew what he had to do and he knew how to do it. Then most importantly, he **desired** to do it with his trusted team members.

He now has four years of sobriety and is living the dream as he often reminds me: happy, fulfilled and successful as a certified mechanic. He also practices and lives an $H_2G/365$ plan every day of his life!

There is absolutely no pause in life's hectic pace like reflection time. You are feeding, healing, and building the **Head, Heart** and **Gut,** particularly for your *self.*

Forgiveness is heavy, powerful, and so important for every human being to understand. It usually conjures up a big sigh when the word is mentioned.

Webster defines **forgiveness** as, "The mental, and/or spiritual process of ceasing to feel resentment, indignation or anger against another person for a perceived offense, difference or mistake, or ceasing to demand punishment or restitution."

Forgiveness is really all about setting **you** free. This can be done by addressing and releasing your past so it no longer has control over your thoughts or feelings. It's no doubt one of the most sensitive and difficult emotions for us to deal with in our life.

There are so many benefits to forgiveness. For those who can never forgive, the burden is heavy, often emotionally paralyzing. We must understand that forgiveness has everything to do with your own well-being.

If we cannot learn to forgive, we cannot grow. We remain in a rut absorbed in anger however quiet. Being able to forgive others can be a transformation that can bring peace and happiness within us.

When true forgiveness takes place, we are able to release the disturbing thoughts and emotions that drain our physical, mental, emotional and spiritual well-being. It's never too late. But there is no need to wait until our loved ones or those other meaningful relationships we have are close to their final days on earth and bed ridden before we have the courage to finally give or receive forgiveness.

Begin this journey of forgiveness now. Find the right time and the right place to tackle it. **Your personal freedom is waiting.**

Once we understand, embrace and commit to living a full Head and Heart mindset and lifestyle, then we can add the G in H_2G to the formula.

H_2G
GUT

The third component of H_2G is **GUT.** This area collects all our fears, uncertainty, doubts and chaos.

The **GUT** is our core. It protects and empowers us to tackle and handle *anything* that comes our way. Those *anything's* are those fearful emotional, physical and mental tests.

If our **Head** is sharp and dynamic and actively engaging and living with all its ingredients AND ALL four chambers of our **Heart** are pumping strong and making progress every day, then the GUT will serve to protect us and get us through the wake-up calls, the storms, and all the chaos that will come our way during our lifetimes.

It's the same way "extreme teams" prepare, battle and overcome fear with a mastery of their GUT. Because we have worked so hard to develop and nurture our Head and Heart, we will be best prepared to successfully manage and overcome our fears.

A GUT check is a conditioned exercise of remaining calm, cool and collected during our greatest times of uncertainty. It's also in this area that we know we have trusted and meaningful relationships that will help us survive these uncertainties.

During those *anything* wake up calls and crisis moment GUT checks, we will need to be calm, cool and collected to have a fighting chance to manage and overcome our fears.

If our heads and hearts are strong, aligned and performing at a high capacity, our GUT will tell us: You can handle the extreme stress and pressure; you are prepared for the decisive moment; you can remain calm; failure is not an option; you and your team are prepared for the chaos and prepared to succeed. You will not panic or melt down; **you are never alone!**

You become disciplined, as the military is taught and trained: to **improvise, adapt and overcome**. Emergency medical response and operating teams, military Special Forces teams on mission, and professional and collegiate sport teams realize the importance of the GUT.

The disciplined and trusted team member knows his or her team handles stress better as a team rather than alone, so no one member has to think he or she must carry the whole team. They all know or end up discovering, often through an incredible experience, that a team can perform and accomplish SO much more than they thought was imaginable! You and your team can realize and benefit from the power of the **GUT.**

I will finish this portion with my last childhood story. It is a story about overcoming fear, one that goes to the core of GUT. I call it:

Sink or swim

At the age of eight, after completing two summer swim lessons at the local military swimming pool, Dad said I was now ready to become a "real swimmer." He always said the swimming pool was a place to get chlorinated and the ocean with its surf, riptides, undertows, and big breakers (big waves) was a place to master your swim skills.

Just don't tell that to the great Olympian, Michael Phelps, the greatest swimming champion to ever compete in the pool!

Starting out in the ocean was pure fear. Dad introduced me to riptides and big surf right out of the chute. Being pounded by big waves, swallowed in the surf like a towel in a washing machine and being sucked out by a strong riptide was a scary experience, even in my controlled protected environment. I did however, have one huge advantage in tackling this fearful experience, my dad. He was a water safety instructor and proficient ocean swimmer who always had my back every second of the "boot camp" experience.

My first experience was swallowing too much salt water and being pulled up by the back of my swim trunks after being repeatedly pounded by what to me, were giant waves. It took a couple weeks before I became comfortable in the big churning surf and began body surfing. Like any newly learned skill, it took a lot of repetitive solid practice, competent instruction, and non-stop encouragement to build the confidence to act in the presence of fear and overcome it, all the ingredients in the **Head** and **Heart**!

In my case, with a Marine as my "drill instructor," failure was not even remotely an option. I had a competent and passionate instructor who had a mission. His team member, me, was going to become an accomplished and confident ocean swimmer and body surfer. Nothing short of that was an acceptable outcome. It was only a question of how long it was going to take. With all his disciplined teaching and instruction while I was growing up he always worked on making the challenge a FUN experience even when fear was pre-occupying my brain and running to my gut.

Over the years, I *did* become a strong ocean swimmer and gained a great love and respect for the sea, thanks to my Dad's teaching. Later as a young adult, I really enjoyed my triathlon races and long two-mile pier-to-pier (Newport to Balboa) ocean swims in Newport Beach, California. I will always be grateful for my swimming and surf lessons with Dad.

Dad had two absolute black and white ground rules ("strategic and critical" thinking at work) for the ocean that I live by to this day and passed on to my kids. First, always respect Mother Nature. Don't ever try to compete with her. She is all-powerful. Two, always use the buddy system in the ocean (and in life!). Never, swim alone. If you cramp up, are knocked out, pass out, are attacked by a shark, or swallowed by a wave, your friend needs to be there to help you.

This experience as an eight year old was bigger than life. Without my Dad's coaching, instruction, and encouragement, I would have never overcome my fears of the ocean. What a freedom experience. What a life experience. I could never have accomplished a team achievement without my trusted team member. Thanks Dad.

When it comes to those crisis moments in your life filled with fear and uncertainty, will you have a strong enough

Head and Heart with supporting team members to survive *and* actually succeed, GROW and continue to live a meaningful and fulfilled life within your trusted relationships? That is the key. That's the secret!

During our time with Jordan's drug addiction and near death experience, Ellena and I realized it was the decisive moment and a serious "gut check" for us.

We could have thrown in the towel and given up after being tested and exhausted for seven tough years of addiction and serious challenges. These were challenges that preoccupied our brains and haunted us for years. We decided instead to maximize, leverage and deploy all our H_2G components: **Head**, **Heart** and **GUT** to take and transform us from **Fears to Freedom.**

Congratulations!
You have just digested the three components of H_2G.

It is now time to learn HOW to use H_2G in YOUR life? What is the daily plan? How do I learn to become an agent of change? HOW can we use H_2G on a daily basis to improve our lives, build more meaning and trusted relationships and realize REAL growth, happiness and success?

$H_2G/365$ Plan for life

The **H₂G/365** daily plan for life first begins with your acceptance and belief in all the components of the **HEAD, HEART** and **GUT**. If you are on board with that, you are ready to begin living the **H₂G** lifestyle.

I have told my family and close friends that when they really engage and **LIVE** H₂G on a daily disciplined basis, they will be so on fire, so energized, and so passionate with their personal and team growth that they will feel more empowered than they ever have in their lives.

The H₂G/365 plan begins with your special 30-minute daily **REFLECTION** time in the morning to set your mind for the entire day. Many will spend time in reflection at the end of their day as well.

The H₂G plan is a daily mindful, physical, mental, emotional and spiritual journey of learning and teaching others. Once you make your 30-minutes of reflection time a ritual, an **unbreakable habit**, you are ready to implement the plan. This will allow you to focus on each element of the plan. Doing this gives you the clarity and peace you need to take today's journey. Like getting back in running shape, it takes some time to build your strength and stamina and you need to maintain your exercise regimen if you expect to see and feel the positive results.

We can't live and grow a meaningful life without a hard working brain (Head) with all its critical ingredients and we certainly can't expect to experience a life of growth, happiness and success without all four heart chambers pumping as rhythmically, efficiently and non-stop as the life giving hearts in our chests.

If we are focused and committed to embracing and engaging in what I refer to as a "working brain" and "pure heart," where all four chambers are consistently pumping at full capacity, and the HEAD is efficiently working then we are all but guaranteed to realize incredible growth in our relationships.

The way to do that is to *live* the precepts of H_2G, not just talk about them, but actually **demonstrate** in your daily life to all those team members around you, the components of **Head, Heart, Gut** and ALL their powerful ingredients!

Try this in your office, factory, school or church, on the playing field- wherever you spend the better part of your day.

I will tell you the daily H_2G plan begins with THOUGHT, INTENTION and ACTION. Remember, the key of H_2G is DOING and BEING not preaching. You must BE the change you want to see in others. How do you do that? After your 30-minute time of reflection or day starter routine, you should be ready to begin your journey. Start with walking in the door of your office. From that second on, throughout the entire day, be a PASSIONATE WARRIOR, an agent of change.

Be mentally, physically and emotionally fit. Be enthusiastic and be on fire about who you are (the self you unearthed in your time of reflection). Remember, it all begins with self and your mind.

Setting the example at the office and becoming contagious takes excellent communication skills as a *transmitter and receiver* and an engaged emotional listener.

H_2G begins with one PASSIONATE WARRIOR— you. You spread your energy and enthusiasm to others in near proximity and it goes viral. It is a new way of **thinking** and doing and all of that starts with you, with a **positive mental**

attitude, walking in the door of your office every morning with how you think and behave throughout the day.

Start your day igniting your intellectual emotional fires. Let your contagious positive attitude motivate and inspire you and all those you meet in your day. Take action! What will I do today to use my positive attitude to touch and connect with someone? Now do it!

You may never know how your positive attitude helped that one person, that one team member, or even that one stranger on the day they needed it most. As we know, teams with positive attitudes overcome difficulty and adversity so much easier and can climb, what they thought were insurmountable mountains together.

Think of the **strategic and critical thinker** ingredient in the HEAD. How satisfying it is when we take the time to be a part of a team that has created that new product, plan or service that turned out to be a big game changer? These innovative and creative ideas, products, plans and services do not come when we are complacent and comfortable.

That's why great team leaders, are always inspiring and empowering their team members to be strategic and critical thinkers both in the moment as well as for longer term planning. Take that time, even if it's just 15-minutes in a day, to exercise that creative 3-pound magical brain to be a strategic, innovative, and critical thinker. Step outside your routine. You may surprise yourself and so many team members.

Another critical ingredient that must be exercised is that of the **"full-time student."** It's exciting, especially with new technology, allowing us immediate access to so much information just keystrokes away. It's also within your teammate. We all can learn so much by becoming an open and engaged listener.

Learning is exciting. Learning a new way to do something better, faster, or more cost-effective, is always a growth experience.

You have to commit time to explore, to unlearn and relearn, and feed your brain constantly. These few hours a week are a fraction of the time many people spend in front of their television sets learning nothing. Learning can't stop or slow down after graduation. We need to continue **thriving** and growing at a level where we are pushing beyond our comfort levels to experience real H_2G growth!

This is what you need to DO

Every day you will print out on paper or pull up on your preferred technology: home computer, cell phone, iPad, Nexus, Kindle…your DAILY H_2G reminder identifying the SPECIFIC day of the year. On the next page is the look of this daily reminder plan.

$H_2G/365$

Today's date: _____

Mental

Emotional

Physical

Spiritual

HEAD

Self

Purpose

Focus

Positive attitude

Effective communicator

Core Competency

Strategic and critical thinker

Team player

Relationship builder

Full time student

HEART

Passionate Warrior

Empathy and Faith

Generosity and Gratitude

Reflection and Forgiveness

<u>**Gut**</u>

Fear

List: YOUR Trusted Relationship Team Members…

    Every Day you want to use this H$_2$G daily map to journal all the different experiences (**Mental, Emotional, Physical, Spiritual**) you encountered and the **ACTIONS** you took or **experienced** in each area.

    One example: You may have, or **MAKE** that special day, where you are going to address and engage in forgiveness with a family member or "lost" friend over an experience that has held you back for years. You **never know** on what day that may happen, unless, you of course are ready to make it happen. Once you encounter it or ACT on it, journal it! **"WID"**- Write It Down, as I told my good friend, Terry. At the end of every day, review your daily H$_2$G/365 Plan before placing it in your 3-ring binder or closing out your H$_2$G/365 computer file.

    Now, watch and feel the transformation that will take place. If you WORK at it on a daily disciplined basis, I guarantee you that real and positive growth, happiness and success will be realized and achieved in your life AND for your team members TOO !

Now that you are a student of H_2G and support the revolution to work harder and build more trusted and meaningful relationships in your life with the H_2G model and daily $H_2G/365$ plan, allow me to introduce H_2G into your corporate world. Recently, I had the distinct pleasure to introduce H_2G Team Culture to many corporate executives, college coaches, the U.S. military and many small businesses throughout the country. It was an exciting opportunity and experience. Even more exciting was to see the keen interest of TEAMS and their desire to GROW through building better and stronger trusted relationships in not only their immediate work environment, but at home, with their close friends, community and business acquaintances.

Thoughts to remember for
H₂G -Head, Heart, Gut

- What will you do

on a daily basis, as not only a plan, but a new lifestyle that will allow you to build, improve and grow these important relationships in your life and the lives of others?

- The core of this H₂G plan is:

*Adopting and **living** a passionate and positive: **Head, Heart** and **Gut** mind-set and lifestyle.*

*-Man is but the product of his thoughts. What he thinks, **he becomes. Be the change you want to** see in the world.*

- The **H₂G plan** and lifestyle is based on you and starts with *you*. You are the vessel that will become so competent, compassionate, understanding, and trusted that you will be a powerful agent for change in the world starting one person at a time, starting in your own family, in your job, neighborhood, community and beyond.

-The "H" or Head in H₂G are: **self, purpose, focus, positive attitude, effective communicator, core competency, critical and strategic thinker, team player, relationship builder, and full-time student.**

-The second "H" of H₂G is HEART and its four chambers.

- **The third "G" of H$_2$G** is **GUT.** This area collects all our fears, uncertainty, doubts and chaos.

- The **GUT** is our core. Our Gut is meant to protect and empower us to tackle and handle *anything* that comes our way. Those *anything's* are those fearful emotional, physical, mental, spiritual challenges and tests that inevitably come our way.

-H$_2$G is a 365 day plan:

The **H$_2$G/365** daily plan for life first begins with your acceptance and belief in all the components of the **HEAD, HEART** and **GUT**. If you are on board with that, you are ready to begin living the **H$_2$G** lifestyle on a daily disciplined basis today.

NOTES:

I encourage you to write your thoughts in this space. Make note of some action items you want to remember. This will fire up your Head, Heart and Gut as you begin the H_2G Revolution.

Chapter Five
H$_2$G in the Corporate Culture

The leaders who work most effectively, it seems to me, never say 'I'. And that's not because they have trained themselves not to say 'I'. They don't think 'I'. They think 'we'; they think 'team'. They understand their job is to make the team function. They accept responsibility and don't sidestep it, but "we" gets the credit. This is what creates trust, what enables you to get the task done.

- Peter Drucker

In today's competitive and changing global economy, the top CEO's and company Board Members clearly know that attracting and hiring the best and the brightest employees is no longer their biggest challenge. The real dynamic challenge is to create, grow and openly nurture and endorse a great company culture that will attract, inspire and retain the best of the best team members.

Behavioral science research studies continue to confirm what every top CEO already knows: to sustain strong growth and profitability and rank among the best companies in their market space, it takes more than a solid mission statement. It takes a great brand, a clear set of values, defined strategies and a clear roadmap for success. It must start with a passionate and trusted H$_2$G company. Leaders who continually fuel and drive a company culture supporting not only the passion **within** his/her organization, but a team passion to **deliver** the absolute best and unmatched "Service First" "customer experience—excel.

The visionary corporate leaders, like Richard Branson of Virgin Companies, truly understand it's all about recognizing and caring for their employees or team members as their absolute #1 priority! One of my favorite quotes of Richard Branson's was when he was asked, "What is the key to success in three words?"

His answer, "People. People. People." So simple, yet so many companies say their leadership is falling short in truly understanding "their people".

Richard Branson is a global change agent who understands the power and benefits of a great corporate culture. As a "full-time student," focused on learning, un-learning and re-learning in a complex and dynamic business world that is changing and growing by the minute, he has successfully convinced his team members that their company success is very dependent on each of them being leading agents of change.

Branson is continually inspiring and empowering all his team members to be creative, innovative and striving to be the best they can be and having fun in the process.

Respected leaders, who really connect with team members, clearly understand this can ONLY be achieved with a great corporate culture. A genuine and winning team environment can ONLY be realized when the CEOs openly embrace, nurture, and promote the culture and have cross-department collaboration. IF these employee values and attitudes are everything, then we know this vibrant culture must be real, alive and **growing every day** in the company.

They also know that their biggest company challenge is identifying and developing the secret ingredients in the culture formula for team members to better get along, build and live a vibrant and fun culture, *and to accept new needed changes necessary to stay competitive as a cutting edge brand leader. The secret ingredients can be found in the "H_2G Team Culture" model.*

H_2G Culture: *"A vibrant team environment that creates & nurtures an H_2G "warrior" attitude that is clearly focused and passionately driven to build trusted relationships to achieve personal and team growth, goals, fulfillment and success".*

For the great corporate team cultures to thrive, five key "H_2G"critical trusted components need to be supported and promoted from leadership. They are:

Connection: It's paramount that team members are emotionally and intellectually connected and committed to understanding and living their clear set of values, beliefs, vision, and defined mission. Daily collaboration, cooperation, compromise and inclusiveness is a MUST.

Communication: Effective, open, honest, and transparent communication is absolutely critical to inspire, empower and ENGAGE team members to be passionate change agent "warriors" for creativity, innovation and growth.

Competency: Every team member is totally committed to be the "best of the best" in his or her area of expertise and service. Being fully accountable and responsible for her expertise and performance is foundational to building and maintaining a great culture.

Courage: Each team member is strongly encouraged to be confident and BOLD in taking risk, being vulnerable and standing up not only to support or critique new creative and innovative ideas, but to be courageous every day.

Commitment: Every team member must be committed to unselfishly care for one another. This is an absolute MUST to building strong team chemistry and lasting sustainable growth. Team members caring for one another **are contagious!**

The "H$_2$G" Team Culture can only thrive with exemplary leadership from the top. CEO's must lead by example and be true promoters of their corporate culture to the same degree they promote product and financial objectives/goals. Without leadership, the company is a ship without a rudder.

Every CEO around the world would likely agree that trust, both within their organization and with their customers, is the foundation to building and sustaining a high performing and successful company.

Stop and think for a moment, what is the cost of NOT having trust within your teams, within your organization and with your customers? It's a Huge factor and a HUGE number.

More often than not, the most successful companies we read about today, like Virgin, Qualcomm, Starbucks, JetBlue, Google (the list is fortunately very large), teach and give their employees a phenomenal range of freedom to do their jobs—they know what trust means. Trust is EVERYTHING!

Widely recognized companies like Virgin Companies, Qualcomm, Google, JetBlue, Starbucks, Southwest Airlines and so many small "Mom and Pop" successful enterprises all get it! They have their priorities right. Only AFTER first creating and promoting a culture of dedicated, appreciated and trusted team members can they be truly prepared to passionately and effectively serve the one they really work for—**their customer**!

It all starts with hiring good team members who fit your culture. Going forward, it's all about caring, recognizing and praising team members for their efforts and achievements. Again, remember the meaningful words of William James, "The deepest principle of human nature is the craving to be appreciated."

Worth repeating as well, Mary Kay, founder of the huge cosmetic company empire clearly supports James' position with her memorable quote that should be invisibly tattooed backwards on every team member's forehead so he/she can SEE it every morning in the bathroom mirror:

"There are only two things more powerful than sex and money—praise and recognition."

The top executives, who truly get it, don't wait for the annual holiday party or awards banquet to recognize and praise their good people. It's a **daily disciplined** practice. They realize that the quality of their team and the quality of the H_2G trusted relationships they build and nurture will determine the company's **destiny!**

With respect to teams in the H_2G Corporate Culture, another friend of mine, Robert, who owned and operated an international marketing agency for many years from the late 1970s through the mid-1990s, shared a bit of insight with me one day over lunch.

We were talking about trust and teamwork in the corporate environment. He had 10 very trusted employees who he depended upon for creativity, clear thinking, positive actions, a customer service first attitude and all the other vital aspects of running a highly successful company in a very competitive arena.

Each week, he would gather them all together and they would review the team covenant they had collectively written.

They made this customized covenant as a vital aspect of their corporate culture. It was something each team member reviewed every day individually and then discussed at the end of the week in relationship to their client contacts and interactions among themselves at the office.

As with all of the elements of your H$_2$G/365 Daily Plan, I would encourage you to customize your team covenant and anything we have discussed in this book or in the H$_2$G Revolution to fit your individual corporate team culture.

Below are a few highlights of Robert's company covenant that I want to share with you.

"I understand that my 100% participation in this team effort will help this team take on an energy and a life all its own. I know that being a part of success is more important than being personally indispensable. I recognize that when a gifted team such as ours dedicates itself to unselfish trust and combines instinct with boldness and effort—that team is poised to climb."

"I also understand the dangers of the "me" disease: inexperience in dealing with any sudden success; chronic feelings of under appreciation; paranoia over being cheated out of one's rightful share: resentment against the competence of partners; personal efforts mustered solely to outshine a teammate; a leadership vacuum resulting from the formation of cliques and rivalries and feelings of frustration even when the team performs well."

"I understand exactly where this team is headed and how it will enjoy the process of working toward its goals. Although I realize my compensation will be fair and generous, I also realize that our team is not working solely for money. If this were the case, we would all be motivated to get rather than to give. I understand that I must always maintain a 'service' attitude rather than a 'sales' attitude. I know that even though 'sales' are a very important part of my responsibility, I must approach sales from a problem-solving attitude. I do not sell marketing or advertising for a living, I sell ideas and solutions."

Every team can benefit from creating a covenant that they can all embrace and practice on a daily basis. Start today to develop one with your team.

Thoughts to remember from
Chapter Five: The H₂G Corporate Culture

-H₂G Culture: *"A vibrant team environment that creates and nurtures an H₂G "warrior" attitude that is clearly focused and passionately driven to build trusted relationships to achieve personal and team growth, goals, fulfillment and success."*

For the great corporate team cultures to thrive, five key "H₂G" critical trusted components need to be supported and promoted from leadership.

They are:

-Connection: It's paramount that team members are emotionally and intellectually connected and committed to understanding and living their clear set of values, beliefs, vision, and defined mission. Daily collaboration, cooperation, compromise and inclusiveness is a MUST.

-Communication: Effective, open, honest, and transparent communication is absolutely critical to inspire, empower and ENGAGE team members to be passionate change agent "warriors" for creativity, innovation and growth.

-Competency: Every team member is totally committed to be the "best of the best" in his area of expertise and service. Being fully accountable and responsible for his or her expertise and performance is foundational to building and maintaining a great culture.

-Courage: Each team member is strongly encouraged to be confident and BOLD in taking risk, being vulnerable and

standing up not only to support or critique new creative and innovative ideas, but to be courageous every day.

-Commitment: Every team member must be committed to unselfishly care for one another. This is an absolute MUST to building strong team chemistry and lasting sustainable growth. Team members caring for one another are contagious!

NOTES:

I encourage you to write your thoughts in this space. Make note of some action items you want to remember. This will fire up your Head, Heart and Gut as you begin the H$_2$G Revolution.

Chapter Six
Service First

Connection

Communication

Competency

Commitment

Courage

There are no traffic jams along the extra mile.

-- Roger Staubach
Former star quarterback Dallas Cowboys

After understanding the 7-Step Trusted Relationship LADDER, one needs to know HOW to build and secure the Trusted Relationship. The first step is to realize and accept that it is NOT about "me". It is all about understanding and caring for your "TEAM" member FIRST!

The famous coach John Wooden said:

Nothing can give greater joy than doing something for another.

Once we truly understand that the secret to obtaining individual and TEAM growth and success is NOT about ME but embracing and living a TEAM H_2G model on a DAILY disciplined basis, companies, families, platoons, clubs, organizations and individuals will ALL realize a radical transformation in performance, growth, happiness and success.

Throughout my 28 years in the California real estate lending and business consulting industry, "SERVICE FIRST" has been my mantra. Embracing and passionately living my H_2G lifestyle has given me the opportunity to build trusted relationships and work with so many outstanding professionals in the field.

I learned early on that it was much more than offering competitive rates, making daily sales calls, and working long weekend hours.

Many of us know that buying or selling a home, particularly our primary home, can unfortunately be one of the most frustrating, stressful and unpleasant experiences for everyone associated with the transaction. It can also be a very exciting, happy, and grateful experience! Many critical variables will ultimately determine the real estate experience.

Because of those many years in the business, I wrote a Service First model, which I am going to share with you. As you will see, my model has universal application to **everyone** in **any** business connected and dependent on sales and customer service. Many of my friends in the financial, pharmaceutical and technology industries have experienced the successful benefits of this model as well. It works everywhere.

Having spent so many years in real estate, I will use realtors and real estate professionals to demonstrate the H_2G SERVICE FIRST model. However, as I said, this model can be applied to any business. The only caveats are: you have to have customers and you have to want to provide the highest quality service in your industry. You'll quickly see the universal application. If you are in the business of selling cars for instance, visualize these examples in your workplace.

It all begins with living the "H₂G" mind-set and lifestyle and all the key ingredients! As with any major project, transaction, or mission, there needs to be a TEAM of expert (core competency) members committed to the mission of professionally and competently serving!

After all these years, I'm still taken aback over how many clients and realtors are unclear on just how many critical "moving parts" there are in the whole process, and how much can go terribly wrong if there is a breakdown in **effective communications**, timing, competency level, or commitment.

From the real estate contract, disclosures, home inspection, loan financing, property valuation, termite report, to the escrow, title, tax and legal positions and opinions, every "moving part" is critical and every team member has a very important and responsible role to serve.

In this real estate scenario, the realtor is the head coach and team leader. The owner is the buyer or seller. This obviously would be the same if you were offering cars, computers or clothing to a customer.

The realtor's job tenure, career reputation and growth of their referral business will ultimately rest on how well they and their supporting team members connect, communicate and competently and competitively SERVE each and every client. (You already read my story about Jose and how this humble customer service agent took care of each of his patrons and what that meant to his boss and his entire business.) I don't know about you, but I abhor bad service and I especially have a distaste for any representative, sales or otherwise who is arrogant enough to think that my time isn't valuable, or my input on his or her product isn't worth listening too. There is absolutely no excuse for this kind of attitude.

There is a good reason why **likeable, understood, competent, respected** and **trusted** top performing realtors are so successful and continually earn so many future **opportunities** after serving their clients well and sincerely.

Taken to another field, a person in need of open-heart surgery is unlikely to select a heart surgeon from a nice magazine advertisement or online yellow pages ad. They will carefully select the surgeon from a highly recommended and trusted REFERRAL from their primary doctor or a trusted friend who personally knows of the heart surgeon's reputation.

While someone in need of a basic oil change may be attracted by an online or newspaper special pricing coupon, they're not likely going to risk having major engine repair work completed by just any mechanic. They too, are more than likely going to seek out a **trusted** referral from someone who personally knows and has experienced a mechanic's excellent work.

The most successful realtors, brain surgeons and car mechanics, like all top performing professionals, have built the overwhelming majority of their successful businesses on satisfied clients and trusted referrals!

Every new and seasoned professional and business is looking for that competitive edge and secret formula to attract more customers and clients, build and grow their business, and be the "best of the best" industry leaders in their market year after year.

Years ago in college, I created this "H_2G" SERVICE FIRST performance model, which became the master plan on how I operate in my business world:

The H$_2$G Corporate Culture is: Connection, Communication, Competency, Competitiveness, and Commitment.

These elements are the roots of the tree of Service First. This model has been my driving force in exceeding client expectations every day and has proven to be my lifeblood and winning formula for building trusted relationships and achieving real sustained growth and success.

Over the past 25 years I have had the opportunity and privilege to make a difference by introducing my "5 STAR" model to many sales and service producers and **teams** in and outside of real estate. Learning of their remarkable increased performances and actually being a part of so many of their successes with this model, has been such a fulfilling experience for me.

It does not take long for a rookie, struggling sales representative, or even a seasoned top performer to realize that without a consistent master game plan and a strategic disciplined daily work plan built upon trusted relationships, they will never fully satisfy their client needs and expectations. They will also never come close to maximizing and reaching their own human potential in achieving their goals.

We must always remind ourselves what every successful CEO thinks about every day: **I can NOT do it alone**. It takes a committed and special TEAM to make it happen and achieve desired results.

The **Service First** model all begins with making a real and caring **Connection**! As discussed earlier in my "7 Steps to Understanding and Building the Trusted Relationship," first impressions and likeability are paramount!

People like working with people they like! It is that simple. They also like to hire people they believe are competent in their field and totally committed to service. So many sales people, like so many relationships, who want it all to happen instantly or overnight, too often, rush or force the relationship.

The trusted relationship built on the seven building blocks all take effort, commitment and time to build.

It all begins with the **Connection**. Before we can start to have real effective and meaningful communication with our customer/clients, the rapport, the real emotional connection, needs to take place. We also need to remember and accept that not all connections are destined to work and turn into to a meaningful and trusted relationship. We can't please everyone. There's a good reason corporations worldwide spend tens of billions of dollars a year on very creative television, radio, internet and magazine ads; they want to continue to make that emotional product or emotional company connection with the consumer and instantly win us over as a valued consumer or client.

The marketing and ad campaigns certainly work for Proctor and Gamble, with $84 billion in annual sales, the world's largest and most profitable consumer products company. While they are obviously in a competitive price driven and reliable product brand business, they really are in the "people connecting" business.

While I have personally never had a cup of coffee in my life, I have always admired Starbucks Founder and CEO Howard Schultz' vision, leadership and contributions to humanity. As previously mentioned, I love his company mission statement: *To inspire and nurture the human spirit, one person, one cup and one neighborhood at a time.*

That says it all and that is what they do! It is sincere, it is creative, and it is meaningful and powerful. Schultz has also been credited with one of the most recognizable quotes in the business world saying: *We are not in the coffee business-serving people, but in the people business serving coffee.* Starbucks not only gets it, they have mastered it ONE satisfied customer experience at a time.

Ironically, so many sales representatives are pre-occupied with selling the product, "taking the order" and making the commission, they never make the *people* connection. The result is, they often end up with unfulfilled sales, a lost client (one they never really had), and no relationship with which to build their business.

However, the "best of the best" professionals do get it. I have had the distinct privilege to serve so many of them and their treasured clients. They truly understand it. Every relationship starts with that special **Connection.** It's a caring connection, or as I like to call it, a special "E.T." connection. We all remember Steven Spielberg's iconic and classic 1982 film. *E.T.* where we witness the magical finger and heart glow connection with the 10-year old, Elliot and E.T. Just ask any successful person in sales or customer service just how special that **magical** connection is.

Every prospective client has his/her unique personality. Every professional realtor and sales rep needs to understand his or her client's personality and find a way to connect with it! Once achieved, the personal and transactional **Communication** can begin.

143

In real estate, when buyers and sellers are open to start sharing their true needs and wants, the realtor can begin articulating and demonstrating his/her **core competency**. Consistent, accurate, and *effective* **Communication** from day one through closing is essential.

Communication is so important in life, and effective communication is critical to the successful operation of any business. So forgive me, but I must identify and mention again the most meaningful communication quote I ever came across and goes with my Service First model. Mom always said, *95% of the world communicates, while the other 5% effectively communicate!*

Every client wants to have the most competent professional representing him or her. Without demonstrating core **Competenc**y, one cannot expect to earn opportunity, loyalty, respect or trust. One cannot expect their business to survive long without it either.

If an individual cannot effectively communicate and demonstrate his knowledge and skill set, his real value is greatly diminished and not fully recognized.

In addition to being industry knowledgeable, an effective communicator, a strong negotiator, hardworking and honest, and fully accountable, clients are looking for that **Competent** professional with the **Competitive** edge that brings added value and goes that extra mile in serving them and securing their desired result and outcomes.

It is understood that honesty and integrity are golden! As discussed earlier, there is a reason the Golden Rule is a time-tested principle with universal acceptance. No successful trusted relationships can be built and sustained without it!

In the Service First model, sugar-coating, avoiding, ignoring, or minimizing the real conditions of the market and a specific property will only lead to a problem escrow filled with headaches, mistrust, undo stress, a cancelled escrow and potentially, even an ugly and costly lawsuit.

In the end, even if the escrow ends up closing and commissions are paid, the relationship is understandably damaged and in many cases, it's over. This "one and done" transactional experience is unfortunately all too common in many businesses where NO real relationship has been developed and/or the Service First model has been compromised!

It is obviously very important to stay emotionally connected in any sale. The relationship is EVERYTHING!

The fifth component of the Service First model is **Commitment.** Commitment is always tested whenever the transaction hits a small or serious potential deal breaker hurdle. In real estate, that could be an appraisal coming in less than an asking price, a borrower struggling to obtain final loan approval, misunderstanding of the executed contract, or some serious property deficiencies perhaps not revealed in the property inspection report. This is the emotional **"G" or gut check** time.

For a real estate professional, this is the decisive moment. This is where fear, courage, or both show up on the battlefield. Some will run, hide, and ignore the problem, hoping someone else resolves it, or it somehow just fixes itself or maybe disappears. Others will blow their stack and become angry, combative and unreasonable out of fear that they are going to lose a commission and client.

The **Committed** professional will demonstrate his bold courage to tackle and face the problem head on. He or she will seek to get the facts, clearly understand the problem, obtain other expert opinion if needed, and work diligently to offer or seek a workable compromise and/or solution.

This is where the H_2G mindset and all the skillset and components must be fully adopted and executed. With a committed GUT, being calm, cool and collected, and assuming the **Head** and **Heart** components are all effectively in play, then the fear and chaos that the buyer or sellers are too often faced with, can be successfully managed. The once insurmountable deal breaker hurdles can many times end up being minor speed bumps or temporary roadblocks that can be successfully negotiated and overcome.

When accurate information can be effectively exchanged and cool heads and positive emotions prevail with equanimity, in that state of stability and composure, successful sales are achieved. This holds true in all areas of sales and customer service.

The earned referral is a "gift" from the Heart as outlined earlier in the 3rd chamber of the "H_2G" Heart: Generosity and Gratitude." The highly satisfied seller or buyer, who truly appreciates and values your trusted relationship and results, will always call upon you for your competency, competiveness and commitment.

Passionately living and incorporating the H_2G SERVICE FIRST model on a daily disciplined basis, will lead to building lasting and trusted relationships. These coveted relationships will pay huge personal and financial dividends with many successful transactions, long-term clients, and referrals for a lifetime!

Relationships, reputation, results, repeat customers and referrals.

It ALL starts with building the trusted relationship, growing your reputation, achieving desired results, and earning and receiving the three most important treasures of business: **trust, repeat customers and referrals.** The secret in your successful journey to achieving record sales, distinguished service, and a fulfilling experience is grounded in H_2G...it's NOT about me. When we genuinely care, openly give and faithfully SERVE our client, there are absolutely NO limits to your personal and team growth, fulfillment and success.

Thoughts to remember from
Chapter Six: Service First

Connection

Communication

Competency

Commitment

Courage

-It all begins with living the "H$_2$G" mindset and lifestyle and all the key ingredients! As with any major project, transaction, or mission, there needs to be a TEAM of expert (core competency) members committed to the mission of professionally and competently serving!

-Passionately living and incorporating the H$_2$G SERVICE FIRST model on a daily disciplined basis, will lead to building lasting and trusted relationships. These coveted relationships will pay huge personal and financial dividends with many successful transactions, long-term clients, and referrals for a lifetime!

-Relationships, reputation, results, repeat customers and referrals.

I would like to finish this journey and help you start yours by ending this book with an almost unbelievable story about never giving up in anything you undertake.

This is a true story that incorporates all of the elements, factors, ideas and formulas contained in From Fears to Freedom and the H$_2$G Revolution. It began over 17 years ago…

NOTES:

I encourage you to write your thoughts in this space. Make note of some action items you want to remember. This will fire up your Head, Heart and Gut as you begin the H_2G Revolution.

Chapter Seven
Never Give Up

"When the world says," 'Give up,'
hope whispers, 'Try it one more time.'"
--Unknown

In 1993, I met a man who was to become my very dear friend and team partner, Terry. He was born and raised in the small and historic town of Gettysburg, Pennsylvania, a special place where American civil war heroes are honored and remembered every day.

From July 1, through July 3, 1863, 150 years ago, more men fought and died on the battlefield than in any other battle before or since on North American soil. The Battle of Gettysburg, with 51,000 causalities in three days of battle was not only the turning point in the American Civil War, but the defining moment in American history. It defined who we were as a nation and the sacrifices so many courageous Americans made, all in the cause for the most precious thing in the world—**freedom.**

Gettysburg represents American freedom. It is hallowed and sacred ground on which President Lincoln outlined his vision for a new birth of freedom in his famous Gettysburg Address. His 272-word dedication speech took only two minutes to present on November 19, 1863 at the Soldiers National Cemetery and is recognized as one of the greatest political speeches of our time.

Over three million visitors from around the world, come every year to see, touch and feel freedom in this unique town of Gettysburg, just 70 miles from our nation's capital.

In 1996, I joined Terry on a trip to Gettysburg to meet his family and tour the 6,000+ acres of battlefield and more than 1,328 monuments, markers and plaques. Before I left California, I had no idea what I was about to experience. Within days, I would begin embarking on the biggest, most challenging and fulfilling project of my lifetime. It would become much bigger than a project. It would become a passionate obsession of mine that would soon test my own H_2G, a test that would be unlike any I'd ever encountered in my life. Ultimately, it went beyond the then boundaries of my mind. It was to me, the quintessential example of the adage, *Never give up,* because it so sorely taxed even the strongest goals and dreams I'd ever had. The experience, though it lasted 15 years, was ultimately a living testament to everything my parents had so painstakingly instilled in me growing up, i.e., overcoming fear with real life lessons.

After landing at Washington-Dulles airport on a 5:30 a.m. red-eye from the west coast in the summer of 1996, we made the one hour and 20 minute ride through some of the most stunning countryside I'd ever visited including: Virginia, Maryland and Pennsylvania, to arrive in Gettysburg.

After first meeting Terry's mother and father at their 19th century farmhouse, Terry drove me to one of the most beautiful pieces of country property I had ever seen. Standing on 62 acres on one of the highest ridgelines in Gettysburg, I had a perfect view of the historic battle of Little Round Top across the valley. Off to the right was a shot of the historic Sachs Bridge; built in 1854, which had been used by both the

Union and Confederate soldiers and though restored it is said to be the oldest covered bridge in the state of Pennsylvania.

A special feeling came over me as I gazed out onto the battlefield and valley. It was an actual physical sensation of a word or a concept called freedom that will always be with me whenever I set foot on this land.

After walking the 37-acre woods overlooking the three-acre lake, I was sold. (Yes, it was actually for sale, which seemed a poor choice for someone and a great opportunity for us.)

The owners, the Roman Catholic Diocese of Harrisburg, had used this 62-acre property for high school summer camps and retreats over the years. At some point, they discontinued their use and it stood guard quietly over the battlefield ever since.

The property had an old 10,000 square foot steel Butler building, complete with a run-down basketball court and old rusted out-kitchen. There were eleven 600 square foot cinder block barracks style "cottages" that were all painted in a 1960's pea green color, which surprisingly did have electricity and water. The water supply came from the natural wells on the property. The electricity was supplied by the local utility company, as was obvious with the obtrusive tall telephone poles and ugly black power lines crossing the property.

While the Diocese had installed an advanced septic sewer system years before, the property was now completely run down and overrun with tall grass and monster weeds, but the view was absolutely breathtaking (worth its weight in gold to me.) My parents had started me on a long love of American history at a very young age. Coming to Gettysburg instantly reignited that passion.

To think I was standing on the high ground overlooking one of the most historic battlefields in the world, the place where a new birth of freedom had begun 150 years before. The hair on the back of my neck still stands straight up every time I step foot on this land and look toward the battlefield. I could only imagine how President Lincoln felt when he came to Gettysburg to honor all those who gave the ultimate sacrifice for this great country, demonstrating courage, valor and honor.

Coming down from my initial exhilaration, 24 hours later, we made contact with the commercial realtor and the Diocese's legal counsel to inquire about purchasing the property. Within 48 hours, we signed a contract to purchase and then quickly opened escrow. Within 45 days, Terry and I owned the most beautiful piece of property overlooking the battlefield of Gettysburg. (It wasn't as easy as it sounds, but it did happen.)

After doing further homework, talking to local elected officials and residents and meeting with a local real estate attorney, Terry and I filed our application papers with the local zoning hearing board to get all our approvals and some of our permits. We were applying for a special campground zoning exception status to build under the current rural conservation district zoning.

Everything in those very preliminary stages seemed routine until we got a huge surprise the night we walked into the zoning hearing board meeting. We were "greeted" with cold stares and a combined bitter defiance. It was our first brutal wake-up call. Talk about first impressions. We could tell immediately that hell would probably freeze over before this local zoning board was going to permit any new development on this historic property, land that we now owned despite its history or attachment to the community.

Looking back, Terry and I had no idea that my battle cry, "Never Give Up", would truly become our living mantra for the next fifteen years! It took a decade and a half of thinking, planning, creating, maneuvering, calculating studying, and engineering, along with a very competent legal team to finally see our dream destination get full approvals and blessings from the Township and the Courts. The team effort was a classic case study. It would even be a good course to offer at any university or college in hospitality, zoning, planning, leadership, and "local politics". I think the best classes, would be included in a military leadership and tactical course modeled after the heartfelt words of my favorite British "Never Give Up" leader, Sir Winston Churchill, "You don't win wars by evacuating."

Our entire team was so passionate, committed and positive throughout the long grind, it would be almost impossible to imagine replicating the effort.

It's these kinds of tests, when you are knocked down time after time, with rejection after rejection that makes a normal person ask, "How can I get up and go on? Where will I find the energy and the courage?"

There was a reason the Gettysburg locals called us, "outsiders".

There were more than a few days where fear and anxiety were staring me in the mirror each morning. I would look at myself as I shaved each morning and ask are you going to roll up the tent, give up the fight, and retreat? Or, as my dad would say, "Are you going to take action, face your challenges head on and overcome your 'temporary" road blocks with a strategic plan?"

The decision was an easy one for us. Before the ceremonial meeting was over that night at the zoning board hearing, Terry and I knew that we were going to stay in the battle, bury our fears of rejection and defeat, and engage in an all-out strategic and orchestrated plan to win the campaign and reach our goal. However, even in the most courageous moments, we all have doubts and so even though we knew we would bury our fear, we nevertheless had serious challenges before us.

Many nights as I reflected on what appeared to be an insurmountable project, I would actually read stories of those who battled and overcame extreme adversity their whole lives. Ironically, the one man, who many view as one of the greatest U.S Presidents, made history in this very town after the most decisive battle of any war on American soil. Now, we were in a battle as well, albeit one of a far different sort.

When I reviewed all the private and public defeats President Lincoln had experienced, I had to read them a couple times to really comprehend the magnitude of his personal, business and political life challenges, adversity and losses. Talk about never giving up.

Abraham Lincoln:

-Ran for the legislature in Illinois and was **defeated**
-Entered business with a partner, and when it **failed** was left with debts that he spent the next 17 years paying off

-Fell in love with a young lady, became engaged to her, and then she **died**

-Proposed marriage to another young lady and was **turned down**

-Ran for Congress and was **defeated**

-Attempted to get an appointment to the U.S. Land Office but **failed**

-Became a candidate for the U.S. Senate but was **defeated**

-Became a candidate for the vice presidency and was **defeated**

-Defeated by Stephen Douglas

-Suffered **the loss of two young sons** -- Eddie, 3, and Willie, 12.

Willie's death caused severe emotional devastation, a loss from which Mrs. Lincoln never recovered.

To think this man with all his adversity and devastating losses and defeats, went on to become one of the greatest President's ever to serve and lead our country during one of the its most trying times, is mind boggling—

talk about overcoming fears on the road to freedom.

To keep my passion burning and daily determination strong, I would incorporate this project into my daily 30-minute reflection time. Prayer and meditation gave me much of the strength, hope and faith I needed to stay the course.

I would also read inspirational quotes to give me the courage to keep my chin up and fight on.

Vince Lombardi's words, "All right Mister, let me tell you what winning means–you're willing to go longer, work harder, give more than anyone else," were always encouraging.

The story that really inspired me was Coach Lombardi's presentation before his last corporate audience. He told his audience that he had the key or secret to success in any business. I believe this is one of the most profound and powerful statements about understanding people. He said, "The secret, in a word is **heart power.** Capture the heart, you've captured the person.... Get people to fall in love with your company."

Lombardi and Lincoln were both masters at capturing the hearts of their teams and in Lincoln's case, the entire nation. They were change agents who passionately and positively impacted people, nurtured and built long trusted relationships, and brought unbelievable growth, happiness and success to so many. They were such powerful change agents that they have been indelibly stamped into our history. We need to remember what they did. We may not be captured for the ages in history books, but if we are Passionate Warriors, we can be and we are the powerful change agents we need to be, we will have made our marks upon our teams.

Over the next 15 years, these powerful leaders along with my father, would affect, influence and inspire my daily disciplined mindset to "Never Give Up."

We knew it was going to be a real battle but it was also going to be a great opportunity to learn, to exercise our powers of persistence, patience, and hard work and yet another chance to say we will not accept failure.

The day we purchased the land on July 29, 1996, the rumors were flying in Gettysburg. It was the gossip of every coffee and barbershop. I could almost see the locals having coffee and talking intensely about their perceptions of what might be coming. Some said we were going to build an exclusive hunting club stocked with quality liquors and fine cigars, a sort of "old boys" club. Someone even started the rumor that we would be opening a mental health clinic, which in hindsight wasn't as far-fetched as years before; a mental health group had tried unsuccessfully to get permit approval for such a facility on our land.

Others said we were going to be building a high-rise modern day hotel overlooking the battlefield that would destroy the beauty of the environment. In addition to all the false rumors, there were many local town folks who made it clear that they were NOT going to allow any "outsiders" to come into their town and build whatever project they had in mind. Fear was running strong on both sides.

Even with Terry, having been born and raised in Gettysburg, and being a fourth generation Gettysburgian, he was perceived as part of an outside "entrepreneurial development group" that did not have the local's best interest in mind. But even then, I never in my wildest dreams, thought it would take 15 years before we crossed the goal line. We were guessing a year or two, something we still laugh about.

I knew that the *fear* among the locals, no matter how unfounded, was real and spreading out of control and I needed to address it immediately.

Within the first weeks, Terry and I made the rounds together and started our campaign. We needed to win over the hearts and minds of some key people in town if we were ever going to have a chance of building our dream.. The first order of business was to hire a respected and proven local business attorney. He was there every step of the way and provided some invaluable support and counsel with his trusted relationships amongst the township elected representatives and so many of the locals in town.

I started reaching out to a local area news reporter who was anxious to report the story. Having worked extensively with media in political campaigns and government, I knew it could be your best friend or your worst nightmare. The fearful part was always the unknown, particularly being an outsider from California. I knew we couldn't control the media and our proposal could end up being reported accurately, or with a local unfavorable bias. We never knew until we picked up the morning paper or watched the local broadcast.

After speaking to the reporter, we reached out to the local business leaders in the township to let them know we were not "development monsters" who were coming in to build some overpowering steel skyscraper hotel. Terry's father, Guy, who ran the local machine shop in town knew everyone and was well respected. He certainly helped us set the rumor mongers straight and get the word out that no hunting club or mental health facility was going to be built.

Once again, **fears** were running high and, as we all know, "perception is reality." We needed to understand, address, and make sure the community's fears and legitimate concerns were addressed and dealt with sincerely.

We needed to start **connecting** with the locals to lay the foundation and to start building trusted relationships.

It would take connections, sincere and effective communication, and reasonable design and building accommodations and concessions to win over the hearts of the locals. We also hired a very competent and seasoned civil and environmental engineer who was respected and trusted by the township zoning officer.

Once we finally connected with a strong base of local supporters, which was a long and endearing campaign, we began to see the "flickering" light at the end of the tunnel and eventually accomplished what we had set out to do.

Finally, November 2009, **13 years after acquiring the land**, keeping a positive attitude, battling zoning officials, winning in the courts, winning over the hearts of a strong local township contingent, AND never giving up, we received our initial design, planning, engineering, environmental, zoning and building approvals. (It is important to STOP here for a moment and let that sink in—13 years later!) It then took 2 more years for us to finalize our zoning approval in the Courts and for the Township Board of Supervisors to ratify and approve our final building and zoning plans.

Our trusted team of four partners (John, Terry, Lou and I) along with our builder, civil and environmental engineer, geothermal engineer, architects, planners, attorneys, hospitality consultants, committed staff and plenty of understanding locals, Terry's Mom, Dad and Charlie made our dream destination a reality. **We could not have done it alone!**

It felt like organizing and running three consecutive Presidential campaigns for 12 years running; exhausting, electrifying and rewarding with the victory in our sights. I should add that we hired a local builder six months before he was elected to the Township Board of Supervisors. He always publicly disclosed his conflict of interest working as our builder, always sought out the legal opinion of his Township legal counsel on our project and he NEVER voted on any matter pertaining to our project approval considerations. Allen was a vital and trusted team member. I was thankful that he was an advocate and believed in the zoning and building merits of our development long before he was elected to office.

Nearing the completion of our project we dedicated something very important, something dear to my heart—in honor of all the American service men and women who fought and died for our American freedom, I had a 40-foot flagpole erected in the center of our property.

Old Glory flies there now 365 days a year, 24 hours a day. At night, when coming back from downtown Gettysburg, I will often pull off to the side of the road, get out of the car, and just stare at it for a few moments and **reflect.** It's always a special moment.

Our united and committed H₂G Team, with hardworking and committed **Heads,** passionate and pure **Hearts** and battle tested **Guts,** persisted on a long journey to eventually end up victorious.

I will forever be **grateful** for everyone's persistence, and hard work. I am also grateful for all the new meaningful and trusted relationships we established over the years with so many of the area professionals and local township residents.

Chapter Eight
Join the Revolution

Individually and collectively with our **H₂G Teams,** we know that we'll never be able to eradicate illegal drugs, lock up or take out all the bad guys in the world or cure all the mental and physical illnesses and diseases in the world. However, we can start today, with one passionate and positive thought to take our first step to begin our journey to forever change and improve our lives.

It all starts with an **H₂G mind-set, lifestyle and a daily disciplined plan** making sure we, along with all our trusted team members, put on our protective battlefield helmets and shields every day with a focused and positive "Head," a passionate and pure "Heart," and calm and collected "Gut." we can begin the journey one disciplined day at a time!

Starbucks CEO, Howard Schultz and his team, are passionately implementing and living their mission statement on a daily basis when they strive to inspire humanity one person, one cup and one neighborhood at a time. If Starbucks, on a massive international scale, can continue to successfully achieve this goal, I believe our small and large teams can inspire humanity one person, one relationship, and one team at a time. Let's be **change agents** responsible for building REAL relationships that matter and are lasting!

The REVOLUTION has begun...

To inspire humanity one person, one relationship, and one Team at a time by adopting and LIVING a passionate and positive H₂G, Head, Heart and Gut mental, emotional, physical, spiritual mindset with a daily disciplined plan to build trusted relationships to achieve individual and team growth, fulfillment and success.

A long but important sentence that captures everything I have been talking about from Trusted Relationships, The Power of Teams, the H₂G Corporate Culture, Service First and beyond.

I hope that you are now on board with the H₂G Revolution and that you will start today to become a powerful Agent of Change within every one of your teams from your one on one teams like your spouse and you, your business, community, churches, everywhere you want to develop a Trusted and Meaningful Relationship.

All of what I've been saying comes down to **choice.** Approach every day of the rest of your life as an essential choice: Today, I will begin by reflecting for a half hour on who I am, what my teams are, how I can be a passionate warrior and how I can contribute to all my teams as a difference maker.

Remember as you begin your day that FEAR is not an obstacle; it is an opportunity we are all lucky to have. It is something that everyone faces and it is something that absolutely must be managed, overcome and used as an ally.

That is why this book is entitled: *From Fears to Freedom*. Remember Nelson Mandela's comments when he said he never felt fear or felt imprisoned, he only felt complete and unequivocal freedom. He had no choice as to where he lived of course, but he still had the freedom that peace of mind brings.

Remember that MISTAKES are temporary setbacks, are an essential part of our everyday lives. It is through fear, mistakes, and setbacks that we learn. It is through these vehicles that we progress and grow if we take the time to analyze them for what they are.

After you have reflected each morning and you are setting out about your day whether that's going to an office, or like the South Coast Plaza Walking Group, you are gathering with one of your teams to talk, to help, to contribute and to begin your day of affecting change. **Be the change you want to see in this world**.

Remember that the H2G Revolution is a 365-Day a year plan that you customize to your own circumstances. You can use my template here to print out your own daily version. Embrace the H2G Revolution today. Take ACTION today, every day, one day at a time!

I shared my "wakeup call" with you. Have you had yours? Will you wait to become an Agent of Change in the world until you do have one? What will you do with your 86,400 seconds today? Think about it.

Are you going to walk out into the world today a mediocre, self-indulgent individual with no particular idea about how you are going to affect those teams around you positively? Or, are you going to wake up with a jolt of understanding and desire to start one hour, one person, and one relationship at a time to help you and all those around you to start the journey out of FEAR and into FREEDOM?

You'll remember early in this book how I spoke of, The Relationship Ladder: 7 Steps to Understanding and Building the Trusted Relationship and how you can go from being likable, to understanding, to being competent, focusing on opportunity, respect, trust and then UNCONDITIONAL TRUST all through your own efforts within every team you are a part of.

You'll also remember that the essence of why trusted teams are so important, is that YOU CAN NOT DO IT ALONE. You may think you can, but you can't!

Review the pages on H2G now. Try to "internalize" and "inculcate" right down to your bones, the aspects of Head, Heart and Gut. That will remind you why you have **choices**—because you have a mind and free will. Every moment of every single day of your life, you have choices. Most are small, but some are large and very important. Right then and there, when you are faced with a fear or an unsavory option, just remember, you have a CHOICE and that choice resides in **your** mind. Remember that Nelson Mandela spent 27 years making choices in his mind standing or sitting in a small jail cell somewhere. He chose to be FREE.

Remember, the major components of Head are: **self, purpose, focus, positive attitude, effective communicator, core competency, critical and strategic thinker, team player, relationship builder and FULL TIME student.**

This is extremely important: No matter how much you **think** you want to be an Agent of Change, you must first find your own deep passion and begin to live a **purpose driven** life.

As you go about your day, think of the Heart in H2G. The Head and the Heart must be in sync. The four analogous chambers of the Heart are: **The Passionate Warrior, Empathy and Faith, Generosity and Gratitude** and

Reflection and Forgiveness. Exercise your HEART every day.

The third aspect of H_2G is the **Gut.** The Gut is your core. It is meant to protect and empower you to tackle and handle anything that comes your way; anything that challenges your Choice and your Resolve: Physically, mentally, emotionally and spiritually. Life is a daily test of your Gut and your courage. It is meant to be that way just like fear, mistakes, and temporary setbacks, are part of our learning and growing process. Without challenges, we slip into mediocrity. At all times, remain cool, calm and collected. Remember, stress is a perception. One person's stressor is another person's ho hum. To the woman who is afraid of flying, getting on an airplane is a perceived stressor. To the woman who flies weekly on business, it is a ho hum. Perceived stressors are nothing more than implanted ideas that can be overcome with a little work.

In the corporate culture, a vibrant team environment creates and nurtures H_2G Passionate Warriors with a

CONNECTION,
clear COMMUNICATIONS,
COMPETENCY,
COURAGE AND COMMITMENT.

In the Corporate Culture, H_2G must thrive from the top down AND the bottom up and it all revolves around our last chapter—Service First. In the Corporate Culture, relationships, reputation, results, repeat customers and referrals are the name of the game.

As you begin your journey with your customized H_2G 365 daily plan remember, not every day will be rosy. Fear will always raise its ugly head. Mistakes and challenges are inevitable but both are vital components to your growth.

I spoke above about "perceptions" and I wish to end on that note. Everything in life is a perception. When you are faced with a "monumental" challenge or problem or fear, remember, that event is coming to you through the prism of your experiences, your upbringing, and your history. It is only a perception and because **you have CHOICES,** you can choose to perceive everything differently—one person, one relationship, one team at a time.

Your ability to make choices in everything you do and think is at the heart of your own H_2G Revolution. If your decisions are "love based" meaning you are always trying to "do the right thing" then your heart is as pure as any human can be. Use the four chambers of your H_2G Heart in every decision. Think before acting. Take a deep breath and count to ten. **Be a Passionate Warrior**; see your choice with **Empathy and Faith. Be Generous and Grateful** and when it's all over, good or bad, **Reflect and Forgive**.

If you made a bad choice about yourself, then forgive that man or woman in the mirror. If you've made a poor choice that affects others, take the time to reflect and rectify accordingly. Apologies are the sign of a Passionate Warrior. Poor decisions are no more than mistakes—they can be managed and overcome.

Through your daily $H_2G/365$ Plan, your ability to make choices and with the help of your trusted, meaningful relationships, you will discover what true peace of mind is and you will be FREE in the most absolute sense, a freedom that no one can take from you, a sense of fulfillment, happiness and success—all right there in your HEAD, your HEART and your GUT!

Make The H₂G Revolution your life time journey!

Never let fear detour or destroy you.

Never think you are alone.

Never think you have to do it alone without your trusted team members.

Never think your failures, mistakes or setbacks are final— they are not!

Never let fear overwhelm you and cage your heart and mind.

Never give up your beliefs and what you know is right.

Never give up your dreams.

Never underestimate your positive influence as an H₂G change agent.

Never forget your trusted and meaningful relationships are EVERYTHING !

Full endorsements

"Shawn Cassidy and I have a lot in common. The focal point of his new book From Fears to Freedom is the power of trusted relationships—and the #2 value at our company is Relationships. We rank order Relationships just behind Ethical Behavior (#1) but in front of Success (#3) and Learning (#4). Why do we rank Relationships before Success? Because we believe you can't have a successful organization unless you build trustworthy relationships with your colleagues, your customers, and your community. Read this book and discover why trust—and relationships—really matter."

- Ken Blanchard, coauthor of The One Minute Manager® and Trust Works!

Shawn's work is powerful and life changing! His life experiences, lessons and shared life principles, clearly demonstrate WHY trusted relationships are everything in our life. This book shows us why Trust is the heartbeat and lifeblood of successful personal and business relationships. His H_2G lifestyle formula is a great "HOW TO" achieve personal growth, fulfillment and success in all areas of our lives.

-Christopher McDonagh, Managing Director

Deutsche Bank Securities

A POWERFUL TOOLBOX FOR CORPORATE AMERICA!

The message discovered in Shawn Cassidy's **_FROM FEARS TO FREEDOM –The H₂G Revolution_** is explosive! How can any team in corporate America be built to drive success in its business without the emotional and professional health of each one of its team members? This "health" is key and exemplified in the 7-step ladder! Shawn's message is concise and crystal clear about what these key ingredients look like in the context of trusted and meaningful relationships which drive success at each turn. Team members using this H_2G formula as a daily methodology will undoubtedly unleash the potential of any organization. It will be no small accident that personal fulfillment will also result from the H_2G approach! BONUS!!

Joni Laura, Senior Director, Legal Counsel

QUALCOMM MEMS Technologies, Inc

From Fears to Freedom is an absolute "must-read" for EVERYONE who desires meaningful and trusted relationships in their lives. This insightful book confirms that no individual or Team can achieve peak performance or any real success without trust. Shawn's "call to action" plan for every family, work, sports, social and spiritual TEAM to join the H_2G Revolution, will truly "inspire humanity, one person, one relationship and one team at a time".

-Thomas L., Special Warfare Operator Chief (SOC)

SEAL, United States Navy (RET)

Shawn's concise discussion of the importance of team building and head, heart and gut health is truly refreshing and inspiring! Healthy relationships are Everything! My personal experience confirms the need for the "passionate advocate" who leads by example. This book provides all the basic ingredients and disciplined formula for taking that first important step in transforming your life.

- John Randolph Backman, MD, FACC, FACSM, FACP - Sports Cardiologist & Marathoner

A powerful and intuitive book!!!! Shawn Cassidy's "From Fears to Freedom" gives a personal account of how to live with PASSION and PURPOSE using the H2G model. Embrace and practice H2G daily and transform your experience, change your life and build success through lasting relationships. Shawn inspires us all to be agents of change.

-Tara Jelley Danielson, Head Field Hockey Coach, Stanford University & former USA National Field Hockey Team Player